AF593553

B-41
"A Native Son" of the San Bernardino Mts.
At Big Bear Lake, Calif.

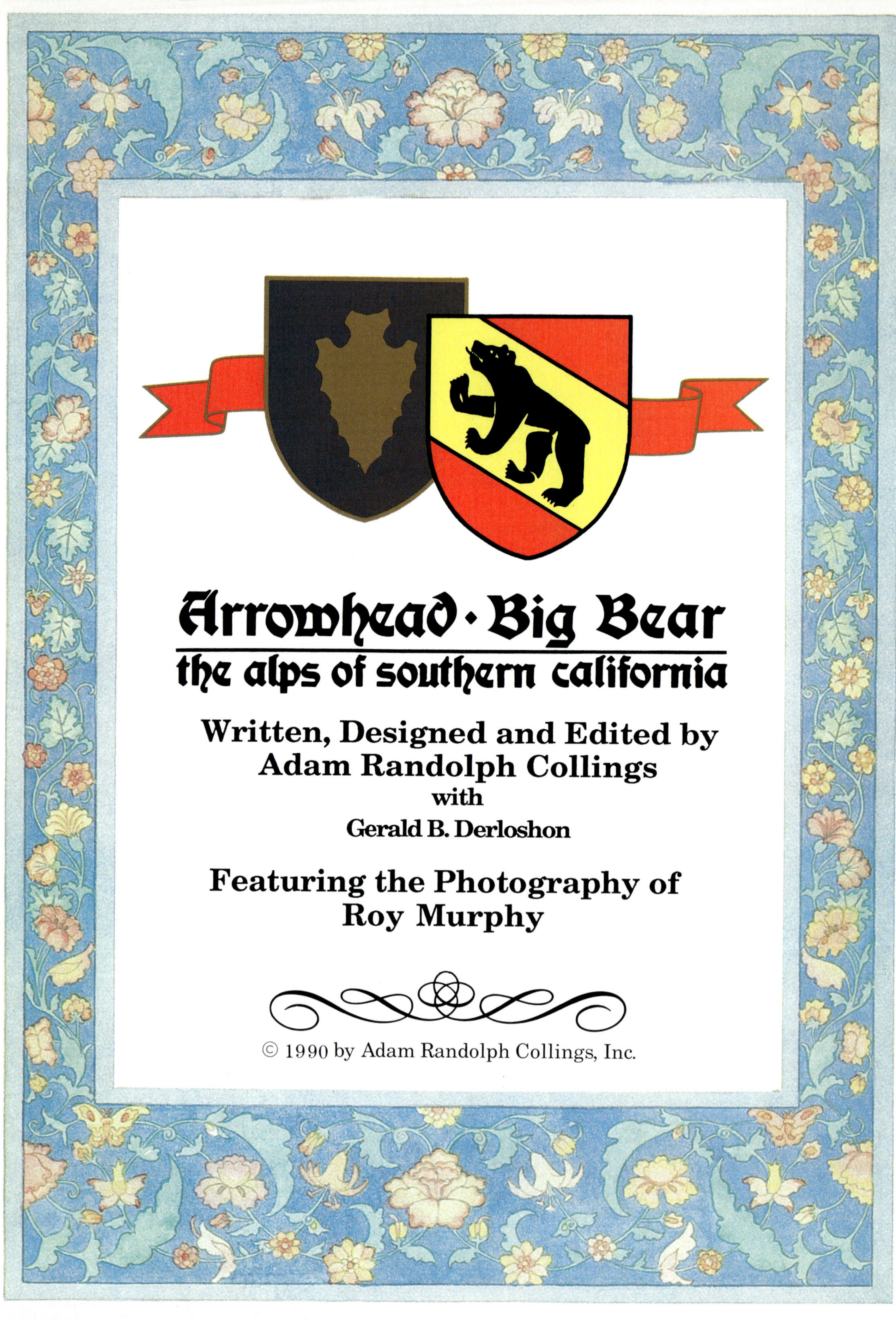

Arrowhead · Big Bear
the alps of southern california

Written, Designed and Edited by
Adam Randolph Collings
with
Gerald B. Derloshon

Featuring the Photography of
Roy Murphy

FRONTISPIECES IN ORDER: Mt. San Jacinto towers above Southern California's Colorado Desert at 10,831 feet. A Quintessential alpine scene at Lake Arrowhead. High Country Meadows at Chilao. All photographs by Roy Murphy. Front Cover: Highest peak in the Southland, Mt. San Gorgonio rises 11,502 feet above California's coastal plain - photograph by Roy Murphy. Back cover: ''Bavarian'' charm at Lake Arrowhead - photograph by Tony Kerst.

Arrowhead Mountain
BOOKS

Published in the United States
by

ADAM RANDOLPH COLLINGS
incorporated

BOX 8658 • HOLIDAY STATION
ANAHEIM, CALIFORNIA 92812

Library of Congress No. 89-092581

"Thousands of tired, nerve shaken,
over-civilized people are beginning to find out
that going to the mountains is going home;
that wildness is a necessity; and that
mountain parks and reservations are useful
not only as fountains of lumber and irrigating
rivers, but as fountains of life."
- JOHN MUIR, 1901

"The Alps of Southern California" – MARK SWAN

The Greater Lake Arrowhead/Big Bear Ecosystem, herein referred to as the Alps of Southern California, comprises both the Transverse and Peninsular Ranges (actually fragmented plates loosely connected to California's Sierra Nevada Mountain Range).

Totaling more than 1,000,000 acres, these mountains encompass the largest tracts of non-desert, undeveloped, wilderness lands in Southern California.

Confronted with the encroachment of urbanization, this high country affords metropolitan Los Angeles and environs a priceless legacy to be appreciated, studied, and preserved.

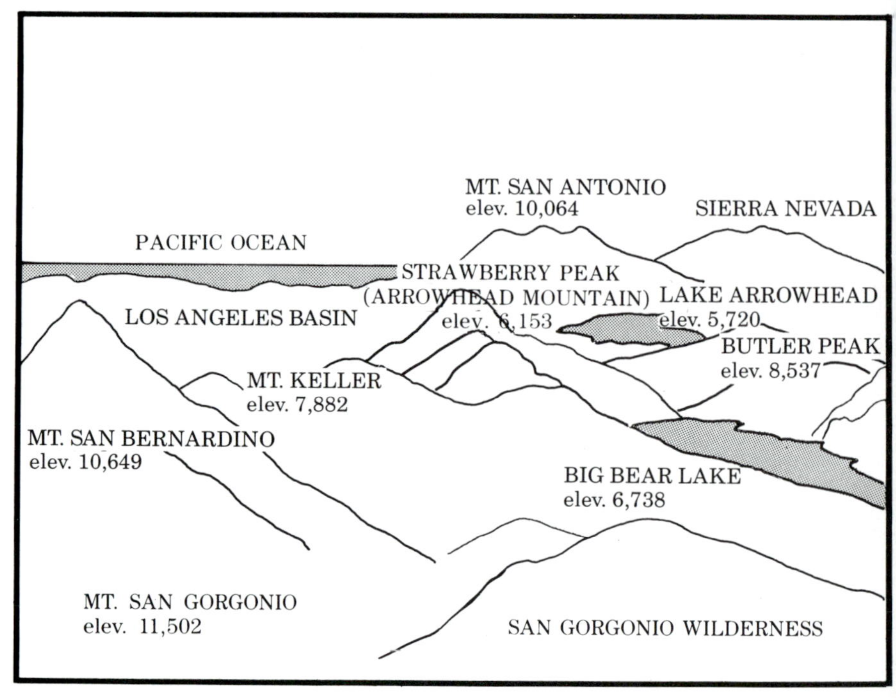

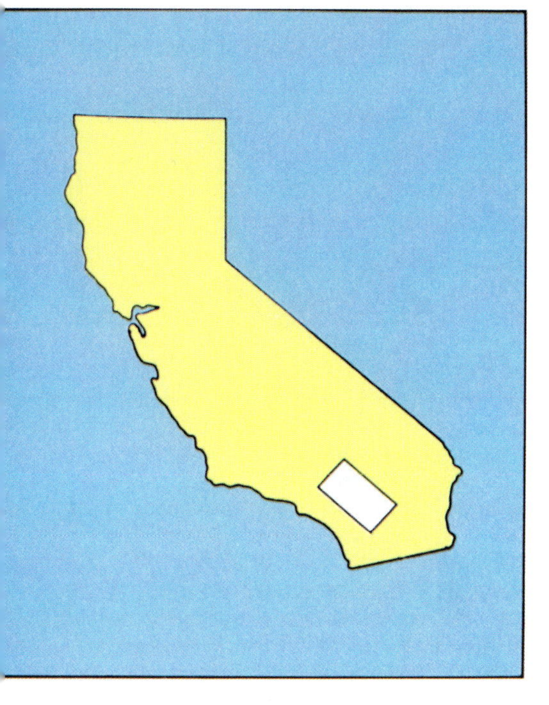

It is characteristic of Southern California mountain chains that when viewed from below they seem austere, barren, and uninviting. Clad in dull green coats of short, shaggy chaparral, which appears threadbare in spots and quite worn through where naked rocks and earth stare gauntly out, these mountains of the south strike one at first as half-starved poor relations set down at the foot of California's regal Sierra Nevada at whose head the snow-crowned Mt. Shasta presides. Innumerable stark gulches and canyons furrow the treeless outer slopes from crest to foot; and here and there from one of these, cleft deeper than its neighbors, issues a gravelly, boulder-strewn wash of the sort that Spanish Californians called an "arroyo" or small river.

To discover the full story of these grand old mountains, to unveil their true beauty, one must follow the arroyo or small river towards its source in the living heart of the hills; and so, seeking to know the river, you come into the revelation of these mountains—an unsuspected world of noble trees and lily gardens, of fern-draped cliffs and alpine lakes and cascading streams.

Granite-bastioned and buttressed, this southernmost extension of the Sierra forms a colossal natural barrier that effectively shuts off the desert and its withering influences from the fertile coastal plain of which Los Angeles is the metropolis. Stretching nearly two hundred miles in length and twenty in breadth its crest stands over a mile high, sporting peaks of well over 10,000 feet. Capstone of the great massif, Mt. San Gorgonio towers like a stone god, overlooking the southland at 11,500 feet above the level of the sea. From such heights down to 4,000 feet one experiences superb views of dense timber, open, sunny forests, and meadows where deer, grey squirrels, and mountain quail live in happy camaraderie, though not in perfect security for bobcats, foxes, and mountain lions are by no means unknown.

Winter storms, which precipitate rain upon the foothills and valleys, frequently descend in snow upon the elevations above 3,000 feet (or occasionally even lower), to melt quickly, however, upon the passing of the storm, except upon sunless, northward facing slopes and in the true high country above 9,000 feet. During about half the year no precipitation of either rain or snow is to be expected, barring an occasional thundershower.

Though at the very edge of one of the most highly developed and populous sections of North America, the Sierras of Southern California are still a very wild land. Only trails traverse its interior. Yet progressive citizens clamor yearly for automobile highways to penetrate the Sierra's silent places and put Switzerland out of business. When they do, startled Echo will add to her repertoire the strident honk of the automobile horn where now she knows only yelp of coyote and bark of fox.

Adapted from a text composed by Charles Francis Saunders for his now classic "The Southern Sierras of California," originally published in 1923 by Houghton Mifflin Company, Cambridge, Massachusetts.

Foreward

"Everywhere you look in California," wrote famed conservationist John Muir, "mountains are ever in sight, charming and glorifying every landscape." Geologists maintain that if mountains were words, California might be considered to possess the world's widest vocabulary. Within its 158,693 square miles, these mountains of the Golden State sport glaciers, waterfalls, geysers, granite monoliths, and alpine meadows, while fully one-fifth of the State is blanketed beneath mountain forests. Few other regions on earth are more diverse or alive in natural splendor. Every ridge, every bend in the trail, every curve in every highway unfolds a new mountain world full of scenic wonders. Only Alaska lays claim to more mountains, yet not even Alaska can boast of such a variety of mountains as those which exist throughout California.

Truly, more than any other feature, save the Pacific Ocean, mountains affect and dictate environmental circumstances within the State itself. Because of them, Los Angeles frequently lies buried beneath inversion layers. Without their benevolent watershed the richest agricultural empire on earth would not exist. And what of world-class ski resorts, redwood forests and spectacular landmarks such as that of the Yosemite? Unlike any other place on earth, here a jaded commuter, traveling the world's most sophisticated freeway system through a complex landscape of high-tech urbanity, can gaze up through the haze at perpendicular slopes and remember what wilderness is. Like balm to the wound, stress is relieved—the anxiety cured.

Anyone familiar with them realizes how little is actually known about these imposing mountains of California. Amazingly enough, they remain to a great extent undocumented. They are simply too many and too vast to accommodate a simple register of elevations and place names. Covering thousands of square miles, together they harbor the most remote of terrain in the American West.

A good deal of the more spectacular of these escarpments tower directly above metropolitan Los Angeles. Within miles of America's second largest city lie alpine forests, stark granite peaks and an abundance of big game. To explore this paradox one but need read on . . .

KING OF THE MOUNTAIN (right) Angeles National Forest.

ROY MURPHY

Introduction

Technically referred to as the Transverse and Peninsular Ranges; historically known primarily as the San Gabriels, San Bernardinos, San Jacinto and the Santa Rosas; poetically described as the Alps of Southern California; this great, timbered vertical wall forms the southernmost extension of California's famed High Sierra. Bisecting and beautifying an otherwise arid, Mediterranean landscape, these mountains harbor an alpine wonderland rich in frontier heritage; ultrascenic in high country splendor.

This is Hollywood's Switzerland and refuge to the urban weary population of America's largest metropolitan area. Visitors here are struck by the singular, unexpected beauty of these most unique of mountains. Towering thousands of feet above deserts and coastal valleys, frequently shrouded in fog, aloof in their stone grandeur, they are truly in and of themselves a world apart—removed and distant from all that surrounds them.

Unlike the rest of Southern California, here one experiences each of Nature's distinctive four seasons. Deep winter snowdrifts yield to flowering meadows in spring. Summer ushers in warm days, blue topaz skies, and star enhanced nights as moonlight dances across the lakes of Big Bear, Arrowhead, Gregory and Silverwood. In autumn, crisper weather brings on the sound of wood being chopped while grey squirrels gather acorns.

Here too one encounters the southland's most abundant legacy of wildlife; a sanctuary to bighorn sheep, black bear, mountain lion, and deer. Great expanses of these mighty bulwarks remain pristine, locked safely away in government-designated wilderness and national forest lands.

Today world-class resorts adorn this once remote high country, affording a year 'round playground for winter and summer sports enthusiasts. To the thousands who now live in the alpine villages that are to be found tucked away amongst these "grand old mountains" and to the millions who visit them each year, the highlands of Arrowhead and Big Bear provide islands of forested paradise floating peacefully above, and worlds removed from the sea of cities and deserts below.

QUAKING ASPEN (left) San Bernardino National Forest.

ROY MURPHY

THE FOREST IS A PECULIAR ORGANISM OF UNLIMITED KINDNESS AND BENEVOLENCE THAT MAKES NO DEMANDS FOR ITS SUSTENANCE AND EXTENDS GENEROUSLY THE PRODUCTS OF ITS LIFE ACTIVITY; IT PROVIDES PROTECTION TO ALL BEINGS, OFFERING SHADE EVEN TO THE AXEMAN WHO DESTROYS IT.

BUDDHA, 525 B.C.

"THE CLEAREST WAY INTO THE UNIVERSE IS THROUGH A FOREST WILDERNESS."
—JOHN MUIR

Arrowhead · Big Bear

the alps of southern california

It was timber that first brought man into these mountains. What he found was a primeval climax forest of pine, fir, and oak towering skyward in dense stands above verdant fern-shrouded meadows, canyons, and valleys. This was the legacy of a not so distant Ice Age when copious amounts of rainfall inundated a now desert-like Southern California allowing for the establishment of woodlands to rival those of today's Pacific Northwest. Quick to locate the grandest of these old-growth woods, within a few years following their discovery more than a dozen sawmills were busy screeching away. The giants were felled and reduced to so many board feet of lumber. Finest timber in the Southwest, it was these forests of the San Gabriels, San Bernardinos and San Jacinto which built the first American settlements in then Spanish Southern California. One mighty tree in particular, symbolic of all, an exceptionally tall, straight lodgepole pine, was toppled on Arrowhead Mountain and ceremoniously marched into Los Angeles amidst the hymn-singing and trumpet revelry of the Mormon Battalion. There it was erected upon a hill overlooking Fort Moore and adorned with the first American flag to fly over what is today a world capital and second largest city in the United States.

Few were those who thought beyond the needs of the moment. A dynamic frontier economy was fueled by the unbridled exploitation of an American West rich in natural resources. Yet, any given resource has its limitations. As slopes and valleys were denuded by the axe, industrial fires raged unchecked across the mountain range, destroying much of that which had escaped the timber barons. By the dawning of this century little remained of the grandeur that had greeted American settlers a mere fifty years earlier.

It was fortuitous indeed that at this crucial moment in time the tide of human events began to change. An enlightened American society came to recognize the inherent value of that which they were about to lose forever. The far-reaching effects of their ambitious industrialization had come to the forefront of social consciousness at the very moment when the fate of American wilderness hung precariously in the balance. A cry went out for preservation rather than exploitation. Were it not for the tireless efforts of the likes of John Muir, Theodore Roosevelt, and a cadre of other standard-bearers the natural beauty and priceless resources of the West would have vanished. Be-

ROY MURPHY

cause of such efforts we today enjoy a land where forests have again begun to attain their former glory, where wildlife still grace mountain landscapes, where the high country remains a wild place little affected by the hand of man.

GARNER VALLEY IN THE SAN JACINTO RANGE

"THE CHRISTMASSY SCENT OF EVERGREENS PERFUMED THE AIR. MAJESTIC WHITE FIRS TOWERED ABOVE US. 'WHITE FIRS NEED AT LEAST 20 TO 30 INCHES OF WATER A YEAR,' ROGER SAID. 'THESE GROW HERE BECAUSE OF THE RELATIVELY COOL TEMPERATURES AND HIGH LEVEL OF MOISTURE AT THIS ELEVATION. THE MOUNTAINS CREATE THEIR OWN WEATHER. EVEN ON THE HOTTEST SUMMER DAY THERE'S SOME MOISTURE IN THE AIR, AND AS AIR RISES UP THE SIDES OF THE MOUNTAINS, IT CONDENSES INTO THUNDERHEADS. YOU'LL BE SITTING IN THE VALLEYS, DRY AS A BONE, AND LOOK UP TO SEE HUGE BLACK CLOUDS RAINING DOWN ON THE MOUNTAINS.' "

—SUZANNE VENINO
NATIONAL GEOGRAPHIC

Pushed heavenward by colossal forces beneath the earth's surface, the Alps of Southern California tower stupendously above a rich, fertile coastal plain. It is here that the Great American Southwest comes to an abrupt halt. Timbered walls, not unlike those of fictional Midian, they constitute a spectacular boundary line, effectively shielding coastal California from the searing heat and seeming desolation of the desert. From their heady heights one can gaze eastward into the classic landscapes of the American West or to the west and south into legendary California. A geographically unique province, they constitute one of but a few major mountain ranges in the world to run east to west, rather than north to south. Primary among such ranges are the Alps of Central Europe. Like their more famous Swiss comrades, the mountains of Southern California are composed primarily of massive granite blocks. Movement along attendant earthquake fault lines has subsequently tilted these enormous blocks upward. As a result, one side of any given mountain in the chain will tend to rise at a gradual slope only to drop off abruptly on its opposite side. In some places these sudden escarpments rise over 10,000 feet in only a few miles distance.

Unlike their famed European counterparts, the Alps of Southern California stand at a more southerly latitude. Their east-west configuration leaves them vulnerable to a full day of sunshine as opposed to the half day experienced by ranges running north to south, causing them to appear noticeably drier than those of Switzerland, Austria and Germany. Yet while chaparral and other brush unique to Southern California covers lower elevation coastal facing slopes, a truly alpine ecosystem exists above the 4,000-foot level where winter storms and the Pacific fog belt nurture dense stands of tall timber. Most spectacular of these are those which adorn the slopes of Arrowhead Mountain.

Desert woodlands of pinyon pine and western juniper grace the more arid lower elevations of the north slope. These in turn give way to sage and creosote as the bounty

of the Alps approach not the lowlands of the Palatinate but rather the great basins of the Mojave and Colorado deserts.

ifty million years ago, during what geologists refer to as the Tertiary Period, North America experienced a far warmer, more humid climate than that to which it is accustomed to today. Temperate forests, rich in both conifers (pine and fir trees) and broadleaf deciduous (oak, alders, sycamore . . .) trees blanketed most of the continent from the Arctic Ocean south to what is now the northern United States. Most of the trees found today in the predominately deciduous woodlands of the East and the coniferous woodlands of the West were well represented together in this all-encompassing primeval forest.

South of the great forest, a mixed subtropical landscape comprised of plant species sharing both northern and southern affinities stretched across what is now the heartland of America. Beyond this middle forest melting pot, semiarid conditions prevailed.

As the Tertiary Period progressed, two major natural events occurred which profoundly, though gradually, transformed this well-ordered landscape into the highly complex and diversified geography that greets us today. First came the slow uplift of the great mountains for which the American West is famous – the Rockies, Cascades, and Sierra Nevada. The rise of these ranges effectively cut off precipitation to lands east of the mountains, creating great "rain shadows" to be cast across the interior of North America.

Increased aridity brought the demise of woodlands as it fostered proliferation of vegetation adapted to desert conditions. Grasslands thus migrated inward towards the center of the continent from points south. Ultimately the eastern and western branches of the ancient continental forest came to be severed completely, by this ever-advancing expanse of prairie lands and desert.

The second major event to alter the face of the land was triggered by a gradual cooling of the planet, which caused northern or boreal forests to shift southward along migrational avenues provided by the newly uplifted mountains.

WHITE FIR

WHITE FIRS ARE LARGE FOREST TREES STANDING 60 TO 200 FEET TALL. THE CROWNS OF MATURE SPECIMENS TEND TO BE ROUNDISH WHILE THOSE OF YOUNG TREES ARE PYRAMIDAL. BARK ON THE TRUNK OF MATURE TREES IS DEEPLY FURROWED AND ASH-GRAY. BARK ON UPPER BRANCHES AND ON YOUNG TREES IS SMOOTH AND GRAYISH. THE WOOD IS LIGHT, SOFT, AND RATHER COARSE-GRAINED. IT IS USED EXTENSIVELY AS DIMENSION LUMBER AND AS BOX WOOD. THEY ARE FREQUENTLY SOLD ON THE CHRISTMAS TREE MARKET AND PLANTED EXTENSIVELY AS ORNAMENTALS.
RANGE: MAIN TIMBER BELT OF THE SIERRA NEVADA, TRANSVERSE, AND PENINSULAR RANGES AT ELEVATIONS OF 3,000 TO 8,300 FEET.

CEDAR RIDGE AT
LAKE ARROWHEAD

"SOUTHERN CALIFORNIA'S ALPS STAND IN A MORE SOUTHERLY LATITUDE THAN THOSE OF CENTRAL EUROPE, AFFORDING A MORE EQUABLE CLIMATE — GENERALLY MILD WINTERS, EXQUISITE SPRING AND FALL, AND A DELIGHTFUL, TYPICALLY SUNNY CALIFORNIA SUMMER, ALL SET AMIDST THE GRANDEUR OF MOUNTAINS AND FOREST."

—A. COLLINGS

At the beginning of what is referred to by geologists as the Ice Age—about three million years ago—boreal vegetation had retreated as far south as Southern California.

Separation of eastern from western forests resulted in the evolution of different species of trees sharing common ancestors. Many types vanished altogether from one forest or the other as a result of severe climatic oscillations. One great chill after another gripped the continent. In the West, amidst the formation of glaciers, the hardy conifers of the Canadian north thrived while most deciduous hardwoods all but disappeared.

Final glaciation climaxed some 17,000 years ago by which time the boreal forest had established itself completely throughout the highlands of the Southwest. Ten thousand years ago the climate had begun to warm rapidly. The present distribution of vegetation throughout the mountains of Southern California represents a gradual adjustment to the generally warmer, dryer conditions that have prevailed since that time.

Today in the Alps of Southern California, conifers form a forest belt ten to twenty miles wide, separating hostile, arctic mountain peaks above ten thousand feet from arid steppes, chaparral and desert sage below three thousand feet. This boreal forest is all but identical to that which extends across northern Europe with one striking variation. Here these woods of the North have been enriched by the addition of numerous species of Mexican origin. This intermingling throughout the Sierra occurred as the same

ROY MURPHY

north-south alignment of attendant mountain ranges provided avenues of migration not only for the boreal forests of Canada but for the subtropical woodlands of Latin America. Here then in Southern California's mountains, where the forests of the North meet with the forests of the South, one encounters a woodland of unequalled richness and variety. Boreal firs and hemlock, together with oak and pine of Mexican origin dominate what botanists have come to refer to as the *Sierra Montane Forests* that adorn these southernmost Alps.

That the Mediterranean gardenlike landscapes of today's Southern California are beautiful is at least predictable. Water in the desert is always beautiful. But the forests at the top of the mountains that tower above this vast oasis are completely unexpected. The long, uplifted, granite block of the San Gabriels, San Bernardinos, and San Jacinto is avalanche-steep and austere. Yet for much of the range the top is relatively flat—at least in comparison to its sides—and cradles many lakes and valleys; large, heavily timbered basinlike areas that remain quite invisible from below.

The dense Sierra Montane Forests of these highland plateaus would seem to belong somewhere else entirely; Douglas Fir, Jeffrey Pine, and White Fir make the traveler feel worlds removed from the typical Southern California

"IN THE HIGHLANDS YOU WOKE UP IN THE MORNING AND THOUGHT: HERE I AM WHERE I OUGHT TO BE."

— ISAK DINESON

MOUNTAIN ISLANDS

Throughout Southern California and the American Southwest one encounters forested mountain "islands" surrounded as it were by a "sea" of desert.

Traveling up the slopes of these isolated peaks and plateaus one enters into a progression of biological communities or ecosystems that duplicate all of the various life zones to be encountered on a cross-country journey from Mexico northward to Alaska. Unique to Southern California is the harmonious blend of these various environments. Overall impressions of a world traveler see arid Saudi Arabia, the foothills of Italy, forests from New England, and high mountains reminiscent of Switzerland. Predominant among such diversity are what scientists refer to as the Transition Zone (south facing slope) and Canadian Zone (north facing slope) Forests which blanket elevations from 4,500 to more than 8,000 feet.

Such elevations experience a moderate climate. Here rainfall of as much as 80 inches a year supports mixed evergreen woodlands together with a variety of grasses, wildflowers, and fern. The Transition Zone stands dominated by yellow pine (mostly ponderosa and Jeffrey) and oak, while the typically more shaded Canadian Zone assumes a distinctly alpine profile with its conical white fir and big-cone spruce.

At elevations approaching 9,000 feet the high, cool forest receives more than twice the precipitation of the deserts below, providing enough winter snow to accommodate the operation of world-class ski resorts. At such heights impressive stands of pine and fir provide habitat for deer and bear. Bighorn sheep grace high, rocky outcroppings that overlook the entire mountain "island."

"Here is nothing to remind one of the sunny desert a half-hour away by car," observed Arizona naturalist Joseph Wood Krutch after driving from valley floor to high country meadow. "Not a plant nor an animal would know how to live in the desert. Most do not even know the desert exists."

landscape which he has traversed to get here. In fact such is the case—he is in a world removed and quite out of synch with its surroundings, for this is a great relic forest.

As warming trends continued, following the close of the great Ice Age, the boreal forests from the North together with the luxuriant canopy of Mexican species since established throughout Southern California began to retreat from an encroaching desert. Today these remnant forests stand, stranded as it were, atop the mountains where abundant precipitation and coastal low clouds continue to nurture them as in prehistoric times. Below and beyond this high mountain sanctuary their coastal and valley comrades have all but disappeared.

That which does remain is truly grand beyond compare. The most diverse conifer forest in the world, it today adorns middle elevation slopes throughout the Sierra Nevada proper as well as in the mountains of Southern California. Although a condition of summer drought is characteristic of this entire region, nevertheless long, warm growing seasons and relatively mild winters combine to create a particularly congenial environment for the conifers that have migrated here. Hence they dominate the woods. On sites where soil is moist and well-drained these pine and fir trees in fact regularly attain record sizes, forming truly impressive forests. Typical stands contain various types of conifers and nearly as many varieties of deciduous trees, the latter albeit as numerous in kind, remaining nonetheless distinctly fewer in numbers.

Just above the chaparral and oak woodlands of the foothills, ponderosa pines form open, parklike forests with grassy floors and scattered shrubs. Here too one encounters an abundance of hemlock (Douglas Fir) and Black Oak. In spring, grasses are green and wildflowers abundant. By midsummer, slopes have been burnished a golden brown.

As elevation increases, the oppressive conditions of the summer drought lift, though not altogether due to the east-west configuration of this range and to its southerly latitude. Forests higher up become denser, richer in species, and profoundly more complex. White fir here is common, along with Sugar Pine and Incense Cedar. Oaks persist albeit on a much grander scale while alders and Pacific Coast Dogwood literally choke the shaded canyons.

Here too one encounters numerous meadows (many now lying beneath the waters of man-made lakes) and upon occasion the beautiful white trunks and shimmering leaves of the Quaking Aspen at this southernmost extension of its range.

Higher still lodgepole pine and alpine fir give way to stunted forests of limber pine.

Upper timberline represents a surrender of trees in the face of increasing cold. Peaks and summits above 10,000 feet are noticeably void of forests altogether as arctic conditions prevail in what scientists refer to as the true *Alpine Zone*.

The lower limit of the forest is a moisture frontier, beyond which precipitation is insufficient to sustain woodlands of any size. *Ripuarian Forests* of cottonwoods and sycamore, however, do descend beyond this lower boundary

PONDEROSA PINE

ALSO KNOWN AS THE WESTERN YELLOW PINE, THE PODEROSA IS ONE OF OUR MOST IMPORTANT LUMBER TREES. MATURE SPECIMENS VARY GREATLY IN SIZE AND APPEARANCE DUE TO VARIATIONS IN SOIL AND CLIMATIC CONDITIONS. UNDER IDEAL CONDITIONS SOME TREES MAY ATTAIN A HEIGHT OF 200 FT. AND A DIAMETER OF 5 TO 6 FEET. BARK CHARACTERISTICS VARY GREATLY FROM LARGE TAWNY-YELLOW OR RUSSET-BROWN PLATELETS TO HARD, DARK, AND DEEPLY FURROWED RIDGES ON YOUNG TREES OR TREES GROWING UNDER LESS FAVORABLE CONDITIONS. RANGE: WIDESPREAD AT ELEVATIONS OF 2,000 TO 8,500 FT. FREQUENTLY IT IS THE PREDOMINANT TREE IN THE AREA WHERE IT OCCURS.

line. Like verdant vanguards of the Sierra Montane Forest belt, they follow the rivers out from the highlands and into the deserts and coastal plains below.

Not surprisingly, wildlife is as diverse and abundant in these southern alps as are the rich variety of coniferous and deciduous trees. Following similar patterns of migration, here denizens of the Northwoods populate an ecosystem together with migrants from the tropical rainforests and highlands of central and southern Mexico.

Most imposing inhabitant of these alps is the California Grizzly. Unpredictable and fearless this great bear, often weighing upwards of 2,000 pounds, posed a serious threat to early settlers, and as such was hunted into near extinction. Today it is estimated that as few as thirty individuals survive, and all of these south of the Mexican border.

A similar tale can be told of the magnificent jaguar who, like the grizzly was hunted down and literally exterminated from these mountains. Last reported sighting of the spotted leopardlike cat occurred above Palm Springs on Mt. San Jacinto in 1929.

Master of the high country is the agile Bighorn Sheep. Two subspecies thrive in these mountains. The Sierra bighorn frequents regions in and above timberline while the more diminutive and starkly colored desert bighorn inhabits the rugged, isolated desert canyons of the Santa Rosa range. Foresters estimate the combined population of both species to be the largest concentration of bighorn

BIGHORN SHEEP

sheep in the American Southwest, with current census at 500 individuals. Conservationists consider this a triumph as the noble bighorn faced extinction less than a hundred years ago.

Black Bear, too, are common here throughout most of the range. Their numbers are estimated at just over 300 animals. Threatened by incessant poaching this most popular of forest dwellers is a delight to behold, but being as unpredictable as brother grizzly, should always be enjoyed from a safe distance. The Black Bear of these southern alps are generally adorned in very dark, dusky brown peltage—not always truly black in coloration.

The mountain lion, too, is still prevalent here. So much so as to have received international attention in the media as an ever-expanding urban population encroaches upon its domain. Today the largest predator in the Sierra Montane Forest, mountain lions may wander as much as a hundred miles across the range on regular hunting forays, often dropping down into the outskirts of desert and coastal communities. Nocturnal and extremely wary of man, this beautiful animal for all of its roaming about, nonetheless is rarely seen by the millions who travel through its mountainous domain each year.

The colorful bobcat, so named because of its stubby tail, is somewhat more conspicuous and less elusive. His dusky coat sometimes appears amber, almost orange in color. Much smaller than the mountain lion, who often exceeds six feet from nose to tip of tail, the bobcat is famed for its nerve-wracking scream and hunting prowess.

The Mexican Grey Wolf, once common throughout the Southwest, is occasionally spotted here in the alps though authorities doubt this presence. By contrast his smaller brother, the ubiquitous coyote can be seen day or night throughout the entire range and beyond. Another animal famed for its voice, the coyote, like the bobcat, has haunted

ROY MURPHY

BIGHORN SHEEP

THE BIG HORN SHEEP (OVALIS CANADENSIS) CAN BE FOUND FROM SOUTHERN BRITISH COLUMBIA TO NORTHWESTERN MEXICO. DESCENDED FROM THE WILD SHEEP OF ASIA, THEY ARE BELIEVED TO HAVE CROSSED OVER THE BERING STRAITS TO NORTH AMERICA MORE THAN 500,000 YEARS AGO.
IF NOT THREATENED BY HUMAN ENCROACHMENT, THE BIGHORNS WILL SPEND ALL OF THEIR LIVES IN A CHOSEN AREA RANGING UP TO 20 MILES. THEY ARE EXTREMELY SELF-RELIANT ANIMALS AND MANAGE TO LIVE AND REPRODUCE IN SOME OF THE HOTTEST AND DRIEST PLACES ON EARTH.

THE YOUNG, BORN USUALLY IN FEBRUARY OR MARCH, ARE ALREADY WELL DEVELOPED AT BIRTH, BUT FOR THE FIRST FEW DAYS KEEP A VERY CLOSE RELATIONSHIP WITH THEIR MOTHERS. BY IMITATION THEY LEARN TO SCALE STEEP CLIFFS, CHEW FOOD, MAKE BEDS IN THE LOOSE GROUND, AND AFTER ONLY ONE WEEK, ARE READY TO TAKE THEIR PLACE IN THE HERD.

many a camper in the wilderness with its midnight serenading.

Outnumbering all other large mammals in these mountains, Mule Deer grace virtually every glen and meadow. Around dusk and at dawn are favored times for sighting this beauteous animal. So named for its large oversized ears, the Mule Deer may stand four feet at the shoulder — bucks sporting impressive antlers.

Raccoons, grey squirrels, chipmunks, ground squirrels and countless other small mammals populate the forests and clefts of these mountains, as do an amazing and colorful variety of birds, reptiles, amphibians and fish.

uring the Ice Age, much of the world's oceans were withdrawn into huge frozen polar ice sheets, causing the level of the sea to fall. Shallows became dry land while ancient shores were left exposed. It was then possible for large herds of animals, and the hunters who followed them, to migrate across a land bridge which effectively connected Siberia with Alaska. Prehistorians generally agree that the earliest humans used this thoroughfare in crossing the 50-mile wide Bering Strait to migrate from eastern Asia to North America.

Anthropologists trace man's first presence in Southern California to the last phases of this great Ice Age. Cooling temperatures and generous amounts of rainfall produced deep water lakes in what are now merely "playas" or dry basins. Lush grasslands stretched for miles across present-day deserts providing an ample diet for herds of grazing animals. Huge mammoths and diminuative three-toed horses grazed in present day San Bernardino Valley while giant redwoods graced the canyons of Arrowhead Mountain. Here, perhaps as long as 50,000 years ago, early man fed off the bounty of a rich and abundant land.

Evidence of man's existence in the mountains of Southern California is found in art dating back to this era which he sketched on the rock walls of his caves; crude stone paintings telling of his daily battle for survival. Additional evidence is found in the petroglyphs and pictographs which have been discovered near places central to man's earliest culture – alongside natural, clear water springs, in and around ancient campsites, and on the cliff faces that paralleled his trails.

Aboriginal hunters walked the gently rolling hills and steeper paths which led two miles up from the valley floor to the rock-ribbed roof of Southern California. The reward for such a skyward climb would have been that of exceptional hunting together with the opening of trade routes between tribes of the coasts and deserts.

The dark skinned, ebony-haired Native American Indians grew in strength and numbers. We know of them by the legacies they have left in what little remains of the tribal village sites which they inhabited.

LEGEND OF THE ARROWHEAD

One of Southern California's most recognizable and enduring landmarks is an intriguing Arrowhead formation on the southwestern facing slope of Arrowhead Mountain. Emblazened on the mountainside, the Arrowhead points downward, actually marking the location of famed Arrowhead hot springs. The total area of the landmark comprises more than seven and one-half acres. It is without flaw from barb to barb, and from shank to point, and is clearly and sharply defined as it lies flat and gray against the clear green/brown mountain.

Father Francisco Dumetz, remembered for having given San Bernardino its name, is the first European to have recorded the presence of the Arrowhead. It consists of fragmented white quartz, light gray granite, and light sage. Chapparal and greasewood shrubs surround the gigantic configuration.

No one knows for sure how the distinguished landmark came into being. Concentrated soil erosion, ancient landslides, dozens of fires, or possibly a combination of all three phenomena may have contributed to its existence. Some even suggest that Indians in the area "built" the Arrowhead by carrying light colored gravel from the Santa Ana and Cajon washes.

In describing the Arrowhead and the valley he found so appealing, Fr. Dumetz wrote:

"The valley seems fertile and there is an abundance of water both from the springs in the lowlands and from the stream flow from the mountains to the north and east. The valley will be found in a one-day march east of here (Mission San Gabriel) and is easily located by a mark on the mountain forming the north rim of the valley.

"This mark is in the shape of a large arrow, after the fashion used by the Indians of the region. It appears to be of natural origin and at the base of the mark is found a hot spring and some mud sinks, the hottest water that I have ever seen issuing from the earth."

Legends of the Arrowhead's origin include one that involves the Cahuilla Indians. The exiled peoples had been driven from their homes in the East by warring tribes. According to the legend, after many moons of wandering, the Good Spirit had mercy on His people and guided them to new hunting grounds with an arrow of fire. The guiding arrow at last came to rest on a mountainside with its head pointing downward towards a fertile valley and its attendant health-giving mineral springs:

Then the blessed rain poured down from above, water cooled the parched earth and filled the empty beds of the streams . . . the people drank deep of the streaming waters, and bathing in them, were healed."

Southern California's present day Inland Empire was home to two major linguistic groups—the Mojaves of the desert and the Shoshonean tribes of the mountains and coast (the latter of which consisted of six distinct tribal groups). The Mojaves lived primarily along the Colorado River east of the mountain range. Known to be peaceful among themselves, they were nonetheless most aggressive in terms of raiding and looting other tribes. The Mojaves traveled regularly down the Colorado River to trade with the Yuma Indians of the Sonora Desert. The Mojaves' interest in trading with coastal Indians resulted in the establishment of a pathway across the great mountains to the tribes inhabiting the more temperate regions by the Pacific.

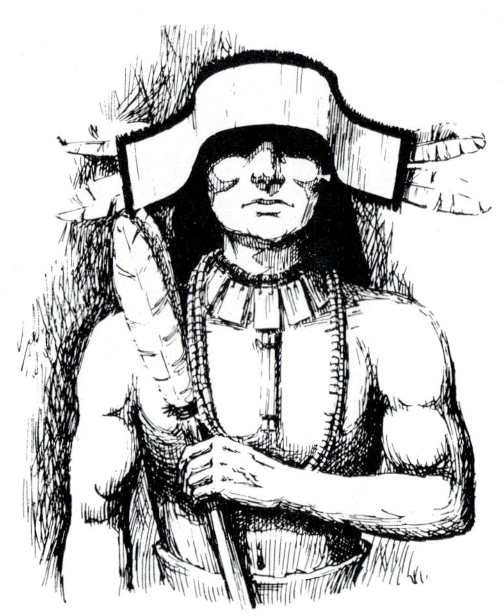

SERRANO INDIAN

Among the Shoshonean tribes of the coast were Indians whom the Europeans would later call Serranos, meaning "people of the mountains" or "highlanders." Closely related to the Serranos were the Cahuilla.

The Serranos lived near springs, streams and rivers in settlements which usually numbered 10 to 30 dwellings. They hunted bear, deer, quail, squirrel, rabbit, and even the bighorn sheep. They fished for trout, harvested crops, and each fall gathered acorns, a major staple in their diet. They also ate grass seeds, insects, mesquite beans, and wild berries. The Serranos were a peaceful, gentle people who were not easily provoked. Highly regarded as skilled basket weavers they took great pride in the designs which they created. Their settlements are remembered today in towns which bear their names—Yucaipa, Cucamonga, Muscupiabe. The Serranos also inhabited locations in and around the east side of the mountain range as well as in Cajon Pass. This pass was and still is the major thoroughfare through the towering peaks of Southern California's Alps.

To the Indians who lived in and around these mountains the dawning of modern times was an era of peaceful coexistence. The mountains were filled with an abundance of wildlife and unspoiled beauty that modern man can only barely comprehend—a climax forest literally thousands of years old teeming with game.

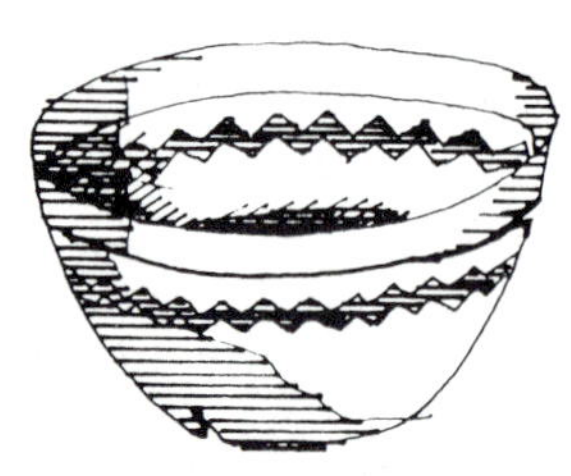

CAHUILLA BASKET

Elder tribesmen among the Serranos handed down an unusual version of the origin of their people. According to legend, two Indian brothers, chosen to become the "creators" of man, held differing views of what man should be like. One thought his eyes should be in the back of his head and that he should have webbed feet. The other felt strongly that man should appear like themselves who looked as man looks today. The two argued violently. Out of exasperation, one finally "left this world," cast out for his bitter-

ness, holding the other responsible for his "death."

Legend maintains that the people designed by the brother who had prevailed first appeared in "the North" and were subsequently led by a great "white eagle" who guided them to what is today known as San Gorgonio Mountain, highest peak in Southern California. The spirit of the deceased brother proceeded to divide these people, however, perpetrating evil from the underworld and antagonizing one tribe to war against the other. This is all said to have happened at *Hatauva,* the "eye of God," a large crystal dome visible in the east end of Big Bear Valley. To escape strife, one tribe proceeded on to the base of Arrowhead Mountain where a mysterious arrow-shaped configuration had been placed upon the hillside as a sign from the gods that they who dwelt there would be protected from their enemies. Unfortunately, gold miners have long since destroyed the unusual natural crystal dome phenomenon, but the gigantic arrowhead configuration and the Indian legend of the origin of the Serranos lives on.

SPANISH CARAVEL
CIRCA 1500

iscovery of the New World by Christopher Columbus in 1492 foreshadowed one of history's most exciting and adventurous periods. During the 300 years which followed, first the Spanish and then principally the Dutch, French, and English would explore the newfound continents that came to be known after a Florentine businessman, Amerigo Vespucci, as *America.* Spanish explorers Hernan Cortez, Ponce de Leon, Francisco Vasquez de Coronado, and the English maritimer, Sir Francis Drake, are remembered for their early and bold charting of the New World.

Sailing under the flag of Spain, a Portuguese maritimer named Juan Rodriguez Cabrillo landed at present day Point Loma, San Diego, on September 28, 1542. Today, Cabrillo is credited as having been the discoverer of California which would soon become known to the rest of the world as *El Dorado* – land of untold wealth.

A single compelling motive drove the Spanish in their conquest of the New World. In a word that catalyst was *gold!* Accounts of vast deposits of gold were embellished at

SIR FRANCIS DRAKE

THE SUGAR PINE

This is the noblest pine yet discovered, surpassing all others not merely in size but also in kingly beauty and majesty.

It towers sublimely from every ridge and canon of the range, at an elevation of from 3,000 to 7,000 feet above the sea, attaining most perfect development at a height of about 5,000 feet.

Full-grown specimens are commonly about 220 feet high, and from six to eight feet in diameter near the ground, though some grand old patriarch is occasionally met that has enjoyed five or six centuries of storms, and attained a thickness of ten or even twelve feet, living on undecayed, sweet and fresh in every fiber . . .

The trunk is a smooth, round, delicately tapered shaft, mostly without limbs, and colored rich purplish-brown, usually enlivened with tufts of yellow lichen. At the top of this magnificent bole, long, curving branches sweep gracefully outward and downward, sometimes forming a palm-like crown, but far more nobly impressive than any palm crown I ever beheld. The needles are about three inches long, finely tempered and arranged in rather close tassels at the ends of slender branchlets that clothe the long, outsweeping limbs. How well they sing in the wind, and how strikingly harmonious an effect is made by the immense cylindrical cones that depend loosely from the ends of the main branches!

—John Muir, *The Mountains of California*

each telling. The Spanish went on a virtual rampage through Central America and Mexico, shipping home shimmering cargos of gold ornaments which they plundered from the natives. Coupled with tales of a "Fountain of Youth," "Seven Cities of Gold," and "terrestrial paradises" where "mermaids and strange creatures lived," the conquistadores came and conquered. They tamed the land they called New Spain. They subdued its inhabitants, the Indians, *converting* them to Christianity and enlisting them into the service of His Majesty, the King of Spain.

THE MYTHOLOGICAL GRIFFIN WAS SAID TO INHABIT THE MOUNTAINS AND COASTAL PALISADES OF ALTA CALIFORNIA.

Traveling with the explorers and conquistadores were Catholic missionaries, many of whom appealed to Madrid and Rome, begging sympathetic treatment for the subjugated neophytes of the Americas. Pope Paul III, responding to protests over the annihilation and enslavement of the Indians, proclaimed them to be "members of the human race." He warned that anyone who persecuted them would risk excommunication from the Church.

It was ultimately this sensitivity to the plight of the Native American Indian that led to the appointment of a Franciscan Friar, Junipero Serra, to serve as spiritual guide under Captain Gaspar de Portola, who was named the first governor of the California frontier in 1767. Spanish authorities ordered what has since been heralded as the "Sacred Expedition" to settle lands to the north of San Diego – lands which they felt might otherwise fall into the hands of Russian fur traders.

The Spanish could hardly have chosen a more worthy padre than Junipero Serra as Indian pacifist. Serra gave himself fully to them. For every fort built to protect the coastline of Spanish California, Serra oversaw the construction of a mission, 21 in all, to protect the souls of the subjugated natives. Of these, Mission San Gabriel Archangel, founded in 1771, is regarded as having been the most economically successful. Its ranchlands extended many miles into the foothills of Southern California's mountain ranges.

FRANCISCAN MISSIONARIES

The first Europeans to visit these mountains were Spanish soldiers in pursuit of rebellious mission Indians. In 1772 Captain Pedro Fages, military commander of the Presidio (Fort) in San Diego, led a group of soldiers in pursuit of neophyte deserters who had fled into the high country. Guided by sympathetic Cahuilla Indians, Fages may or may not have been successful in his attempt to capture the fugitives, yet in fulfilling his duty to the Catholic monarchs of Spain, he secured a place in California history as the first European to cross over the desert pass of El Cajon. Breeching the Southern Sierra, allowing coastal plateau and

Mojave Desert to meet, this pass of El Cajon would become a major thoroughfare between Southern California and all points east of the Sierra.

To the Serrano Indians, the ''highlanders,'' who probably monitored Fages' journey with interest from afar, the Spanish soldiers riding tall, strange, four-legged beasts through the pass would have been unlike anything they had ever seen, native Americans believing upon first sight that both rider and mount were one animal.

The next white visitor to encounter the Serranos was a Franciscan Padre, Father Francisco Garces. Traveling with only Indian companions, Father Garces developed excellent relations among the various tribes on both sides of and in the mountains. Sitting with them for long hours around their campfires, conversing "adequately" in their native tongue, he won them over to his gentle, caring nature.

In the winter of 1776, Father Garces began an extraordinary journey. Having learned that the Mojaves were trading with coastal Indian tribes, Father Garces secured Mojave guides and journeyed with them from the desert across the mountains to Mission San Gabriel. Following the Mojave River upstream into the high country, (not far from present day Lake Gregory), up to the summit and then descending down into the valley below, he became the first white man to have traversed the range itself.

In 1806, Father Jose Maria Zalvidea, newly appointed head of the San Gabriel Mission, followed virtually this same route in crossing the mountains. He visited numerous Indian tribes en route, baptizing as he went and teaching new and better methods for irrigating their lands and constructing their dwellings.

On May 20, 1810, semiretired Father Dumetz, also of the San Gabriel Mission, visited one of the valley's rancherias (Indian villages). While there, he built a small chapel wherein Mass was celebrated. As it was the feast day of Saint Bernard of Siena, Father Dumetz called the locale *San Bernardino.* That name would years later come to identify not only the valley, but a city, a mountain, a mountain range, a national forest, and the largest county in the contiguous United States.

Mission records at San Gabriel indicate that many priests of the day journeyed into San Bernardino Valley. Each recounted that the Indians received them warmly. Nevertheless, due to the remoteness of the mountain tribes and the aggressive tendencies of the Mojave tribes, highlanders and desert Indians were perceived as dangerous. Several skirmishes between Spanish soldiers and Mojave

TULE ELK

CAPTAIN PEDRO FAGES

Indian warriors around 1812 caused a decline of mission influence in the area. But that influence would soon be restored as continued pressure for pastures and farmland brought about the establishment of Rancho San Bernardino near present day Redlands. With its long, adobe-brick room, timbered with beams cut from the local mountains, Rancho San Bernardino became the region's first successful European business venture. Soon other ranchos were established, each the envy of a newly landed Spanish aristocracy.

Life for Southern Californians of the early 19th century revolved around vast herds of cattle, agricultural enterprises, and citrus groves. In the mountains, the Serrano and Cahuilla Indians saw the presence of white men draw ever close, not only from the west where the nightly fires of Colonial ranchos now burned in the valley, but from the east, from whence approached the blonde, Yankee, buffalo-robed mountainmen.

n the early 1800s, the same powerful yearning for independence that American Colonists had experienced some 50 years earlier began to be felt by Mexican citizens longing for self-government. Rumors of a split with the European monarchs spread across New Spain like wildfire. Napoleon Boneparte's 1808 French occupation of Iberia fueled the revolutionary machinery in the New World. After a decade of on-again, off-again uprisings and conflicts between those who wanted self-rule and those who professed loyalty to the crown, Mexico finally secured its independence from the motherland. The year was 1822.

Long regarded as insignificant distant outposts, settlements in Alta California remained far removed and literally unaffected by the political turbulence emanating from Mexico City. In the missions and ranchos of El Dorado no dramatic, overnight transformations occurred. Yet change was in the offing. Men who had set their courses westward from beyond the Rockies would soon turn the idyllic pastoral Spanish California into a chaotic scene of revolution and change.

At 27 years of age, Jedediah Strong Smith had already gained popular acclaim as a legendary figure of the American frontier. The blue-eyed, buckskinned giant matched his muscle and his cunning with hostile Indians

RANCHO SAN BERNARDINO WAS VALUED FOR ITS HIGHLY FERTILE SOIL AND NUTRIENT-RICH GRASSES. ORCHARDS OF OLIVE AND FRUIT TREES WERE PLANTED AND PRODUCED IN ABUNDANCE. GRAZING CATTLE WERE HERDED ONTO RANCHO GROUNDS BY THE THOUSANDS. A 12-MILE LONG IRRIGATION PROJECT IN 1819 BROUGHT MUCH NEEDED WATER TO THE RANCHO FROM MILL CREEK. IT BECAME THE MOST EXTENSIVE IRRIGATION PROJECT OF ITS KIND DURING CALIFORNIA'S MISSION PERIOD.

WITH MORE THAN ENOUGH WATER TO SUPPLY BOTH CROPS AND ORCHARDS, ADDITIONAL AMOUNTS OF WATER WERE USED IN PASTURES. BY 1830, MORE THAN 25,000 HEAD OF CATTLE GRAZED ON RANCHO LAND. THIS FACT CONTRIBUTED TO THE ECONOMIC VITALITY OF THE SAN BERNARDINO AREA AND ESPECIALLY TO THAT OF SAN GABRIEL MISSION, HEADQUARTERS OF THE ENTIRE LOS ANGELES REGION.

LIFE ON THE CALIFORNIA RANCHOS DURING THE 1840S FEATURED LARGE CATTLE ROUNDUPS AND RODEOS, HORSE RACING, COCK FIGHTS, AND BEAR AND BULL FIGHTS.

CATTLE RANCHING PLAYED AN INTEGRAL PART IN THE ECONOMY OF THE REGION AND FOR A TIME, CATTLE WERE BY FAR THE MOST VALUED COMMODITY A MAN COULD OWN.

as handily as he did with angry grizzlies. He braved the rigors and challenges of his incredible travels with the determination of a man on an important mission.

Formerly a partner in the Ashley-Smith Fur Company, Smith led 16 trappers west of Salt Lake en route to the fertile, wooded valleys of the Colorado River in early November 1826. The adventures of Jedediah Smith document an important time in the history of Alta California during its early years under Mexican rule.

Smith and his party were well received by the Mojave Indians who 50 years earlier had guided Father Garces up the river which bore their name. With Indians as guides, Smith followed their lead and Garces' footsteps into the San Bernardino mountains. His band of trappers, wearing their fringed leather buckskins, surmounted the pass, arriving at San Gabriel Mission on November 27. While his men replenished their provisions and made needed equipment repairs, Smith left for San Diego to meet with and attempt to gain favor of the newly empowered Mexican authorities.

After a period of unexplained delays, Smith and his party were abruptly ordered out of the territory. In 1827, with a party of 18, Smith retraced his route across the desert. Once again the Mojave Indians greeted him as a friend. But while crossing the river, Smith and his men were savagely ambushed by the unpredictable desert tribes. Ten trappers died while Smith and several companions narrowly escaped to the safety of the San Bernardino Valley.

Regrouping at Rancho San Bernardino Smith once again replenished his supplies. He continued his journey into Northern California, Oregon, and then back to the Rocky Mountains where the legend of his prowess grew. Today Jedediah Strong Smith is remembered as the first American-born explorer to have traveled overland to California.

CATTLE • THE FOUNDATION UPON WHICH WERE BUILT SOUTHERN CALIFORNIA'S FIRST ECONOMIC EMPIRES.

The Mexicans knew how tentative their grasp was on Alta California. They knew that grasp became even more tentative with the encroachment of men such as Jedediah Smith. In an effort to avoid losing their hold on the land, Mexico imposed a requirement that all foreigners must travel with passports which they made virtually unattainable. Nevertheless, tales of the West Coast's land of milk and honey

CALIFORNIA RANCHERO

“THE STORY OF THE SAN BERNARDINOS IS ONE OF TIMBER BARONS, GOLD STRIKES, AND RESORT DEVELOPERS.”
— A. COLLINGS

spread as Smith and others flung open the floodgates. Ignoring passport laws; motivated by the desire to explore new lands and discover new wonders; western trailblazers continued to press into Alta California.

Soon annual caravans began transporting hundreds of pioneers together with their belongings into the Mexican Territories. Eventually, much to the dismay of Mexican authorities, great herds of California cattle and horses fell prey to maurading bands of renegade Indians who found that they could trade them to the unsuspecting American emigrants for a handsome profit. A lucrative black market developed as violence spread to the rancho and mission lands, with bandidos taking refuge in the remote back country of the mountains.

This outbreak of hostility coincided with the secularization of the missions. It had been the intention of the Mexican government to turn management of the missions over to the Indians. In 1833 mission buildings and land were confiscated from the Church and placed under the rule of government-appointed administrators. Missions subsequently were reduced to little more than parish churches. The lives of the Indians who depended upon the mission societies were turned upside down. Wresting property away from the Catholic Church and turning it over to neophytes wholly unfamiliar with the affairs of business and real estate proved disastrous. The Indians fell prey to shrewd speculators and often wagered away their inheritance for a jug of spirits.

Governing displaced Indians and an ever-increasing population of foreigners who wished to trap, hunt, and even settle in California, was not an easy task for the authorities in distant Mexico City. In 1836, Californios committed a bloodless coup, sending an ineffective Mexican governor packing. It seemed there was a high degree of independent thinking among Spanish California colonials.

Meanwhile, still more trailblazers and adventurers persisted in seeing first-hand what the country "California" was all about. Unlike Jedediah Smith, a Bible-carrying witness to Christianity, some of the West's frontiersmen were of far less honorable character. Peg Leg Smith and the mulatto mountain man, Jim Beckwourth, secured their place in the history of Southern California's mountains by participating in one of the largest and most daring horse-routing schemes ever recorded. Together they stole as many as 3,000 steeds in one night from the ranchos of San Bernardino.

Smith and Beckwourth had aligned themselves with a fierce, young Ute Indian chief named Walkara whose principal trade with the Navajos was the women and children he abducted in exchange for good Indian ponies.

SAN BERNARDINO (SAINT BERNARD) MOUNTAINS

ROY MURPHY

JEDEDIAH STRONG SMITH

Walkara also frequently preyed upon Spanish trade caravans. He soon became warrior leader of a fierce band of Ute, Paiute, and other renegade Indians. Traveling with Smith and Beckwourth on a trip to California in 1839, Walkara seized an opportunity to route 600 horses out of Cajon Pass. A year later, Smith and Beckwourth realized that Walkara's methods had been far more fruitful than their own, and that corralled California horseflesh was easy prey. Together the three men plotted the most daring raid in frontier history.

Traveling with a pack train, Beckwourth slowly and inconspicuously wound his way along the Spanish Trail, through Cajon Pass, and into the San Bernardino Valley. On cue, with the precision of a modern-day military operation, several of Walkara's Indian companions opened the corrals at numerous ranchos and the gates of several large stockades. Under a full moon, Beckwourth and the Indians sent 5,000 horses thundering into Cajon Pass. The stunned Californios reacted quickly enough to maneuver about 2,000 of the horses out of the stampeding herd. Adding insult to injury, while the victimized rancheros were taking a much needed break from the pursuit at a watering hole, Walkara and a few of his men snuck up behind them and managed to steal their horses as well.

A raid of this magnitude completely overwhelmed the Californios. Their work of settling Southern California and the heavily forested mountain ranges which towered majestically overhead, would continue successfully, but the days of peaceful isolation and Spanish dominance on a remote frontier had come to an end.

ith secularization of the missions completed by 1834, the fledgling government of Mexico began transferring title of the Franciscan dynasty to many influential political and military figures. Mission lands were bestowed upon the Lugos, Bandinis, Picos, and Sepulvedas — names which to this day ring familiar thoughout California.

In 1838, Juan Bandini received a 25,000-acre land grant along the Santa Ana River. Bandini, among the first of the grantees to secure timber from the San Bernardino Mountains to build his dwellings, became so interested in his newly acquired forests of pine and fir that he arranged for the first logging road to be built, the *Corte de Madera,* along the Mojave Indian Trail. Others who followed his lead were Benjamin Wilson and Isaac Williams, two of the first non-Hispanic land grantees. One of Williams' young employees was American logger Daniel Sexton. Sexton operated one of the mountain's first primitive sawmills, which he located in San Gorgonio Pass.

THE PASSES

"WITH ALL THEIR INFINITE VARIATIONS THE MOUNTAINS COMPRISE NOT ONLY HEAVING WAVES OF FORESTS, BUT JUTTING CLIFFS, ABYSMAL GORGES AND DEEP SUNLESS CANONS, VAST OPEN PARKS AND TINY ARCTIC MEADOWS, SMALL BLUE LAKES, GUSHING MINERAL SPRINGS, COLD TROUT POOLS, LACY FALLS, HEAVY CATARACTS AND GREAT SOGGY MARSHES, ROLLING HILLS OF SAGE AND CEDAR, HIGH GROVES OF ASPEN, IMMENSE FLAT-TOPPED MESAS, SOLITARY BLUFFS AND WEIRDLY ERODED BUTTES.

YET OF ALL THESE COMPONENTS PERHAPS THE PASSES COME MOST READILY TO MIND. TO ALL LIVING CREATURES, EVEN TO BIRDS SUSCEPTIBLE TO THE AIR CURRENTS ABOVE THEM, THEY HAVE BEEN THE IMMEMORIAL GATEWAYS THROUGH THE MOUNTAINS.

THROUGH THESE DEFILES, FIRST WORN INTO ANCIENT GAME TRAILS BY HOOF AND CLAW, HAVE PASSED THE FABULOUS PARADE OF INDIANS, MOUNTAIN MEN, TWENTY-MULE TEAM FREIGHTERS, CRACK TRAINS AND BOILING FORDS THAT IN ONE CENTURY HAS TELESCOPED OUR ENTIRE HISTORY."

– FRANK WATERS

HIGH MOUNTAIN PASS

MT. PALOMAR RISES ABOVE A CONTEMPORARY CALIFORNIA RANCHO

BENJAMIN DAVIS (BENITO) WILSON

There were other Dons (Spanish gentry) in the valley interested in the valued timber economy of the mountains. Among them was Antonio Maria Lugo who had been granted the former Rancho San Bernardino.

Rancho life during 1834 to 1846 left its imprint on California society to such a degree that we romanticize about it even today. The foods, the music, the festivals and the customs of the Rancho period survive even though the period that spawned them lasted for little more than a decade. It was during this era that the much heralded California lifestyle of today was born: a tradition marked by gracious hospitality and the endless pursuit of pleasure.

Mexican and American traders continued to pour into Southern California in search of strong and sturdy horses and mules. With vast and fertile pastures, livestock grazed to their fill. As many as 2,000 prized horses and mules might leave the San Bernardino Valley during any

ADAM COLLINGS

given year en route to Eastern and Mexican markets. As the local economy continued to grow, so did opportunities to exploit the improved resources. Problems with horse thieves and Indian raiding parties continued. Antonio Maria Lugo and other Dons sought the assistance of the new American settlers in combating the violence which persisted. Continued development of settlements by law-abiding and honest people would be their best defense against continued attacks.

Benjamin Wilson accepted the challenge of maintaining law and order on the Southern California frontier. He became Justice of the Peace for the Inland Territory. Commissioned by Mexican California Governor Pio Pico, Benito Wilson (as his amigos called him) led the region's first genuine effort against lawlessness. His path was soon to cross that of the feared, and by now legendary, Chief Walkara.

"PRINCIPAL AMONG THE MOUNTAINS OF THE PENINSULAR RANGE IS A HIGH, ELEVATED PLATEAU KNOWN AS PALOMAR. THIS LOFTY, TIMBERED TABLELAND STRETCHES ACROSS SAN DIEGO'S BACKCOUNTRY, BRIDGING THE HIGH COUNTRY OF MT. SAN JACINTO WITH THAT OF THE LAGUNA MOUNTAINS."

—A. COLLINGS

CALIFORNIA GRIZZLY

"FOR NOW WE LEFT THE WARM, OPEN WORLD OF YELLOW SUNSHINE FOR THE COOL BLUE SHADOWS OF THE FOREST. SQUIRRELS CHATTERED OF OUR COMING FROM THE SHAGGY PINES.

THE TRAIL NARROWED, STEEPENED. WE WOUND UPWARD SINGLE FILE, STOPPING FREQUENTLY TO REST THE HEAVING HORSES. THE YELLOW PINES GAVE WAY TO DOUGLAS FIR AND LODGE POLE PINE TOWERING SIXTY, EIGHTY FEET HIGH. A DEEP, ANCIENT AND MYSTERIOUS FOREST, LIKE A WELLING DARKNESS THROUGH WHICH ONLY A TRICKLE OF LIGHT DROPPED FROM ABOVE.

AT THE BOTTOM OF THE CANON FAR BELOW, A STREAM POURED WHITELY, FEATHERING AT NUMEROUS FALLS, THEN SUBSIDING INTO STILL TROUT POOLS AND BEAVER DAMS. JUST PAST MIDDAY WE STOPPED FOR LUNCH IN AN OPEN GLADE. THE SUNLIGHT SEEMED PALE AND WEAKENED WITH ALLOY, AND OUR FIRE FELT COMFORTABLY WARM."

– FRANK WATERS

In 1845, Walkara pulled off a devastating attack against a large herd of Lugo-owned cattle, driving them off into the desert. In pursuit of Walkara, Wilson led a group of New Mexicans and Californios on the chase. He sent half of his men through Cajon Pass and the other half into San Bernardino's Santa Ana Canyon. Climbing higher and higher over steep ridges, the latter party came upon an alkali lake and a small Indian settlement surrounded by forests of tall Ponderosa and Jeffrey Pine. Instead of locating Walkara however, they discovered a large number of grizzly bears foraging in the open. Abandoning their concerns about renegade Indians, Wilson and his men made good sport of throwing their ropes around the necks and feet of the grizzlies, playing with the great bears as cats might play with mice. They took 11 huge pelts that day. Word of their adventure in what immediately became known as Bear Valley spread.

The following day, Wilson picked up the pursuit of Walkara. He came upon four Indian braves, one of whom was the Indian outlaw, Joaquin. Wilson's musket felled Joaquin but not before the outlaw managed to shoot a poison arrow into Wilson's shoulder. Benjamin survived the encounter, saved by his friend, Lorenzo Trujillo, who sucked the poison from the wound. Wilson and his party returned down the mountain where news of the discovery of a Valley of Bears overshadowed the fact that once again Walkara had escaped.

It would not be until 1855 that Walkara's reign of terror would close, when the chief fell victim to blood poisoning. Barbarian to the end, he had ordered that two Ute wives, two strangled Indian maidens, one live Indian boy, sixty horses and six sheep accompany him on his funeral pyre.

The ongoing problem of protecting each other from raiding Indians and white outlaws became the Californios' dominent concern. Of increasing concern to the Mexican government, however, were the many American "squatters" settling in the northern part of Alta California.

Most Californios were sympathetic to the Americans but understandably held strong Mexican ties. Former friends, such as Don Lugo and Benjamin Wilson, often found themselves on opposite sides of the political fence. Yet most strove to maintain a position of neutrality.

The Treaty of Guadalupe-Hildalgo in 1848 brought to an end a war which had claimed the lives of Davy Crockett, Jim Bowie, and thousands of brave men on both sides. In the treaty, California and much of the Southwest was ceded to the United States. As outlined in that treaty, land ownerships legally recognized by Mexico were likewise recognized by the U.S. Government.

The Californios of today's Southern California saw an economy based primarily upon livestock gradually shift to one dominated by agricultural enterprises. Hispanic culture merged with that of the increasing number of Americans coming westward via the Spanish Trail. One particular group of newcomers — the Mormons — would have a significant historical impact on Southern California as well as upon the towering forested mountains that comprised its most stunning geographical feature.

ormons came to Southern California in the service of the United States Army intending to fight against Mexico. But alas, they arrived in the San Bernardino Valley (after having completed the longest infantry march in recorded history—from Council Bluffs, Nebraska) only to find the war already ended. For the Morman Battalion, their new orders were to help maintain peace among the desert Indians and the Californios. From their appointed positions in Cajon Pass, they soon became acquainted with the Los Angeles basin. It did not take them long to discover that from the head of the Mojave trail, eastward and again to the west, for miles, extended a dense forest where pine, fir, and incense cedar grew tall and straight. Word spread fast among Mormons beyond the desert to the east about the beautiful coastal valleys, their congenial people, and the high mountain timber reserves.

MORMON SETTLERS

Meanwhile in 1848, gold had been discovered at John Sutter's Mill in Northern California. Never before or since have more people uprooted their lives so completely as they did during the California Gold Rush. Fortune seekers came from every state and territory in the Union as well as from scores of countries around the world.

The man who carried the first official news of the gold strike out of California was none other than Kit Carson. Traveling by way of Cajon Pass, official U.S. Government correspondence which Carson carried gave full details of the strike. That letter was the basis for a subsequent news story in the *New York Herald,* and soon the known world focused its attention on the western slopes of the High Sierra.

When Mormon Battalion Captain Jefferson Hunt realized it was too late in the year to lead a group of eastern gold seekers over the Sierra range, he chose to take his expedition into California via the Salt Lake Trail (formerly the Spanish Trail). With more than 100 wagons in tow, many of the travelers grew impatient. Against Hunt's advice they split off the trail to find a shortcut over the Sierra Nevada. For all of them, Death Valley far outmatched their strength and endurance. Many died along the way. Hunt, meanwhile, together with the rest of his party moved on to San Bernardino Valley and ultimately north into the goldfields.

"A MIX OF ELEVATED PLATEAU AND PEAKS, BREACHED BY 2 DESERT PASSES, THESE ALPS OF SOUTHERN CALIFORNIA CONSTITUTE THE STUPENDOUS BOUNDARYLINE THAT EFFECTIVELY SEPARATES LEGENDARY CALIFORNIA FROM THE DESERT LANDSCAPES OF THE AMERICAN SOUTHWEST."

— A. COLLINGS

Thereafter Hunt's Southern route became popular among Easterners coming into California. San Bernardino Valley was a place where travelers could recover from the hard desert crossing. Isaac Williams frequently served as host to trail-weary travelers, especially to Mor-

mons, and he seriously entertained selling his land holdings to them.

In 1851 the leader of the Mormons, Brigham Young, reluctantly approved the establishment of a Mormon settlement in Southern California's San Bernardino Valley. While he saw the agricultural opportunities as being rich and important, he was nevertheless concerned about the number of "saints" who lined up to go on a journey that would take them far away from his Utah headquarters. Historical records list that 150 wagons, 588 oxen, 336 cows, 21 calves, 107 horses, 52 mules, and 437 settlers departed the Salt Lake area in March, 1851.

After their arrival the Latter Day Saints, as the Mormons called themselves, camped in Sycamore Grove while their leaders negotiated purchase of Rancho San Bernardino from the family of Don Antonio Maria Lugo. Thereafter a site was chosen to become the city of San Bernardino. Working earnestly, the Mormons built a secure stockade on the site of the present day courthouse at Arrowhead Avenue. As they planted their crops and orchards and built a fledgling community, their activities in the valley called for an ever-increasing need for good lumber.

Lumberman Daniel Sexton supplied much of the valley with timber. He hand-hewed and pit-sawed most of the lumber that was taken down the mountain. But many Mormons, seeing their needs outpacing the ability of the lumberman to furnish adequate quantities and prices, decided to tap the rich timber resources themselves. In their energetic ways, the Mormons carved the first real road up into the west end of the San Bernardino Mountains. Called appropriately the Mormon Road, it took 10 to 15 days—1,000 man-hours—to build. After following Hot Springs (Waterman) Canyon to its end, the road then climbed its way to the summit of Arrowhead Mountain.

By the end of 1854, six sawmills were busy in the high country producing the finest timber in the Southwest. Agricultural harvests were equally productive. In an effort to protect their political interests and to assure their "theocracy in the wilderness," the Mormons lobbied for and obtained the creation of what became and still is the largest country in the United States. Henry G. Sherwood, architect of Salt Lake City, was called in to design the "city" of San Bernardino in this newly formed County of the same name. Such prosperity however would prove shortlived.

Trouble erupted when two Mormons ran for County offices against "church approved" candidates. Following this act of political betrayal against the Church, serious land disputes between Mormon and non-Mormon caused

FELLING A GIANT

Arrowhead · Big Bear

the alps of southern california

further dissension and unrest. Furthermore, calculating the threat of hostilities between the U.S. Government and the Salt Lake Valley Mormons, Brigham Young abruptly recalled from California all Mormon colonists in late 1857. Young never had been personally supportive of the sizeable but independent San Bernardino settlement.

Over half of the Southern California Mormons elected to stay. They, however, were never again able to regain their political influence in the affairs of the County. Neverthe-less, the Mormons had indeed successfully guided the formation of the city and the county, establishing deep-seated traditions of industry and brotherhood among neighbors. Though in power only a short time, their efforts effectively propelled the growth of the region well into the twentieth century.

In the mountains, the tall trees which had stood for thousands of years would stand a little longer following the Mormon exodus. Neverthless, several sawmills continued in operation. For a brief time however, some of the loggers' attention would be diverted from the big trees to the creeks and mountain streams. "Gold!" the cry sounded. Bill Holcomb had found gold in Big Bear Valley.

A MINER'S BEST FRIEND

inding gold anywhere in California following the 1848 discovery at Sutter's Mill in Coloma seemed possible to anyone with even the slightest trace of gold dust in his eyes. By 1855, it was only natural that in the mountains of Southern California miners would dig, sluice, scratch, and pan in search of the precious mineral. Several mining parties were busy near Bear Lake (present day Baldwin Lake) in 1855 where a State Geologist concluded a miner's efforts produced a meager average of about $3 per day.

A man named Joe Coldwell is credited as having been the first person to work a placer mine in a small canyon at the south end of Bear Valley. The area soon became known as Starvation Flat or Poverty Flat in recognition of the paltry $3 to $5 diggings recovered each day.

Some miners in the valleys and canyons of these southern mountains had already tried and failed to strike it rich in the gold fields of the Sierra Nevada. The smarter ones had other vocations to fall back on — merchants, hunters, carpenters, blacksmiths, and lumbermen. William (Billy) F. Holcomb was such a man. Holcomb left his native Indiana for Northern California and Oregon where he spent 10 hard years searching for gold. His skill as a marksman far surpassed his talents as a prospector, however. Any rabbit, squirrel, deer, bighorn sheep, mountain lion or grizzly that Holcomb sighted was as good as dead.

BILL HOLCOMB

After abandoning his prospecting and mining efforts in the north, Holcomb came to Los Angeles where he heard reports that some placer mines in the San Bernardino Mountains were uncovering marginal gold deposits. Unable to give up the dream of one day striking it rich, Hol-

> "CLIMB THE MOUNTAINS AND GET THEIR GOOD TIDINGS. NATURE'S PEACE WILL FLOW INTO YOU AS SUNSHINE FLOWS INTO TREES. THE WINDS WILL BLOW THEIR OWN FRESHNESS INTO YOU, AND THE STORMS THEIR ENERGIES, WHILE CARES WILL DROP OFF LIKE AUTUMN LEAVES."
>
> — JOHN MUIR

comb found himself drawn back to the mountains. The year was 1859. The place was Bear Valley. Holcomb and his partner, Jack Martin, staked a claim.

The winter of 1860 was harsh. Deep snowdrifts piled high. Several miners decided to pack up and abandon the high-country enterprise, but not Billy Holcomb. Struck by the beauty of the mountains and by the abundant game in the area, he relied on his talent with a rifle to earn his keep, supplying loggers, trappers, and other tenacious miners with meat and furs.

In May, while Holcomb hunted bear, he found himself standing on a ridge overlooking a small valley. Descending into the valley, Billy wounded the largest grizzly he had ever seen. Pursuing the giant bear along what is now Caribou Creek, the intrepid marksman was stopped dead in his tracks when he noticed glittering specks of gold in a quartz ledge.

News of Holcomb's find in the valley that would later bear his name spread faster than a canyon fire in the middle of a dry, hot summer. Prospectors began staking and

ALPINE WINTER SCENE
NEAR BIG BEAR

working their claims. Buildings sprung up — Grant General Store, Two Gun Bill's Saloon, Van Buren's Grocery, Van Dusen's Blacksmith Shop, and the famous Octagon House where the "glitter girls" danced and otherwise entertained men in small, dimly lit rooms.

Quartz and stamp mills appeared with astonishing speed, bearing names like Vulture, Grasshopper, Blue Quartz, Metzger, and Gold Mountain. By fall, some miners were making as much as $50 a day, a tidy sum in 1860. Soon Holcomb Valley's population surpassed 2,000. The largest of several towns in the valley was Belleville, named after Belle Van Dusen, the blacksmith's daughter. It wasn't long before Belleville had a larger population than the city of San Bernardino. Some people believe to this day that if a ballot box hadn't been "accidentally kicked" into a bonfire on election night, Belleville would have become the new county seat. As it was, San Bernardino retained its position by a mere two votes.

Sawmilling continued during the gold rush, meeting an urgent consumer need for clapboard and other building

"IT'S ALWAYS MORNING IN THE MOUNTAINS."

—*PAT CREAMER*

THE SIERRA MADRE

Fountains of life, forests harbor one of the greatest reservoirs of biological diversity on earth. At the dawning of the nineteenth century they blanketed the canyons, northfacing slopes, and highland plateaus of mountains throughout Southern California. From them flowed two major rivers, the Mojave and the Santa Ana, together with scores of lesser streams and watershed. Extensive Ripuarian forests attended these waterways out from the heart of the high country across desert and plain. By mid-century virtually all riverside woodlands had been logged off by Spanish colonials. The front range of the San Gabriels together with the foothills of the San Bernardinos had all but been incinerated as rancheros set fire to the chapparel in an effort to expand grazing lands for their cattle. Such uncontrolled burns often raged through foothill and canyon into the high country itself, there consuming the old-growth forest primeval in its wake until extinguished either by rain or snow.

Benjamin Wilson was the first to blaze a trail into the heart of the San Gabriel Mountains. His route followed an ancient Serrano Indian footpath up Little Santa Anita Canyon to the top of the mountain that today bares Wilson's name. Beyond Mt. Wilson the corridor reached Chilao where logging immediately began in earnest. Today virtually denuded, the stark appearance of the towering San Gabriel high country reflects the intense exploitation to which it has been subjected.

It was Abbott Kinney, founder of Southern California's Venice Beach, who sparked a *fire* of protest against the unbridled abuse being inflicted upon these "grand old mountains." From his ranch in Altadena, at the foot of what was then referred to as the Sierra Madre, Kinney launched a campaign to create extensive forest reserves. His efforts instigated a statewide movement towards conservationism that climaxed with the recruitment of famed naturalist John Muir as spokesman.

Congress responded by passing the Forest Reserve Act of 1891 granting authority to the President "to set aside as public reservations public lands bearing forest wholly or in part covered with timber or undergrowth." Subsequently President Benjamin Harrison signed into existence the San Gabriel Timberland Reserve (renamed the Angeles National Forest the following year) on December 20, 1892.

Interest in the San Gabriel Mountains as a resort destination focused on Mt. Lowe where two ingenious engineers, Thadeus Lowe and David MacPhearson, had constructed a breathtaking cablecar together with attendant hotels. In 1904, the Carnegie Institute selected Mt. Wilson as the location for one of the twentieth century's most historic scientific ventures. Atop the summit were erected several of the world's greatest telescopes.

By the turn of the century, multitudes of curious lowlanders inaugurated what Southland historians have since referred to as the Great Hiking Era. Backcountry trail resorts and hunting lodges sprang up throughout the Angeles National Forest and beyond.

PACK TRAIN, SANTA ANITA CANYON

MULE DEER

materials. Virgin pine fell from dawn until dusk as some men "mined" more gold from the trees than in the mills and streams of Holcomb Valley. Along with the population explosion came a pressing need for more and better roads. Jed Van Dusen, blacksmith turned engineer, was hired to build a road down the north (desert) side of the mountain to connect with Cajon Pass.

The Holcomb Valley gold strike of 1860 proved short-lived. The many quartz ledges soon played out. Some people believe that a Mother Lode, the substantive source of Holcomb Valley gold, still lies undiscovered.

In the yellow fever frenzy of the 1860s, Holcomb Valley was fairly equally divided between the law-abiding and the ruthless. Today, visitors who travel the 12.5-mile "Gold Fever Trail" will encounter significant physical evidence of this romantic, bygone era, including Two Gun Bill's Saloon and the Hangman's Tree. It has been determined that about 50 murders took place in Bear Valley during the first 24 months of Holcomb's discovery.

Southern Californians meanwhile felt both the positive

ROY MURPHY

and negative effects of the gold rush. They took the good with the bad. Of greater concern to them than the outlaws—greater concern than even the Civil War—was a severe flood in 1861 and a smallpox epidemic in 1862.

After the war ended, the United States having proved itself stronger than those who would divide it, a period of optimism swept across the entire nation. At the turn of the century, the call of the West lured many in wake of such a promise, to seek out opportunities for a richer life in fabled California.

As ranching and agricultural enterprises, together with their attendant towns and cities, thrived in the lowlands the ever-increasing demand for building materials led many an ambitious young man to look to the mountains for opportunity. One such individual was Frank Talmadge.

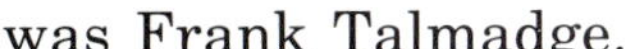

COYOTE

Traveling overland in 1853 from Illinois to Los Angeles, Talmadge took time out from his long desert crossing at the Mormon Fort of San Bernardino to go hunting in the nearby mountains. Like so many since, once Frank reached the woods after his arduous trek on foot up Arrowhead Mountain he discovered what he had come West to find. He was home. Talmadge returned to the mountain in 1862, this time with his wife and six young children. He obtained work as a mill hand and by 1868 had acquired enough timberland to establish his own logging operation, which he did on what is now Point Hamiltair in what was then Little Bear Valley (now Lake Arrowhead).

The following year Frank and his wife, Jane, warmly received a neighbor, William LaPraix. LaPraix was a French Canadian who had come to the mountains in search of Holcomb Valley gold. His entrepreneurial instincts led him to invest his gold dust into a logging operation, which he did across the valley from Talmadge at what is now Orchard Bay.

JOSEPH AND CHARLES TYLER

By 1872 the Tyler Brothers, Joseph and Charles, had acquired a small mill in neighboring Grass Valley. These two industrious young men built their fledgling timber cutting enterprise into a first-class sawmill.

Talmadge, LaPraix, and the Tylers each turned enviable profits while enduring tremendous hardships. Their's is the story of men and women who pitted strength and courage against the mountain; a classic frontier saga reading more like a Hollywood screenplay than true life. These first settlers struggled against the elements, predators, Indians, and occasionally each other. They made their own tools, raised their own food, built homes and furniture, and cut roads through thick forests and up steep canyons. They gave birth, raised families, carried on businesses, and buried their dead without modern conveniences of any kind and yet with few complaints.

SAWMILL AT BLUE JAY ON ARROWHEAD MOUNTAIN

In 1867, displaced Serrano Indians joined the ranks of Walkara's legacy of renegade desert Indians in an attempt to rid the mountains of white miners and settlers. Their raids commenced in Little Bear Valley (Lake Arrowhead) where a band of 60 braves set fire to a sawmill and cabin. Talmadge and his neighbors were quick to respond. Both settler and Indian found themselves caught up in a social struggle too complex for either group to fully understand or resolve. A confrontation occurred near Grass Valley where six traditionally peace-loving Serranos were killed and numerous others wounded. Talmadge and his posse pursued the Indians across the range through Holcomb Valley and eventually out into the Mojave Desert where banished "highlanders" made their escape, leaving behind women and children in a mad dash for survival. Thirty-two days later Frank returned home to his own wife and children in Little Bear to contemplate future attacks. None occurred.

LaPraix would marry only to lose his young bride in childbearing the following year. Ten years of industry and thrift resulted in financial success for the grieving timber baron. He came to be loved and respected by many both on and off the mountain. Then tragedy took his life as well when he fell into the machinery of his own sawmill.

IT'S THE WATER

WRITING IN 1915, USC GEOLOGIST GILBERT ELLIS BAILEY USED SUPERLATIVES TO DESCRIBE THE WATERS OF ARROWHEAD.

"THERE IS AN ABUNDANCE OF PURE, SOFT WATER BUBBLING UP FROM THE GRANITE ROCKS HIGH ABOVE THE HOT SPRINGS BELT, SUFFICIENT TO SUPPLY A LARGE CITY. THESE COLD SPRINGS ARE ONE OF THE MOST VALUABLE OF ALL THE MANY ASSETS WITH WHICH NATURE HAS ENDOWED THIS 'LITTLE WONDERLAND OF GOOD THINGS.'

"THEY ARE NOT ONLY GOOD WATERS LIKE THE HOT SPRINGS, THEY ARE EXCEPTIONALLY GOOD. ONE IS JUSTIFIED IN USING SUPERLATIVES IN DESCRIBING THEM, FOR THEY ARE REMARKABLY PURE, CLEAR, COLORLESS, SWEET WATERS, CONTAINING SCARCELY ANY MINERALS IN SOLUTION."

Joseph and Charles Tyler watched as their logging opperation burned to the ground. They rebuilt and continued to prosper.

Daniel Huston, who had come to the mountains to compete with the Tylers by opening up a sawmill at Huston Flats (now Lake Gregory), was attacked and nearly killed by a grizzly (not an altogether uncommon occurrence during those early days).

By the turn of the century, over a dozen major sawmills were screeching away in the mountains of San Bernardino, San Jacinto, and San Gabriel. Around them grew the towns of Crestline, Running Springs, and Idyllwild.

Insight has been called a "light which lets you see what other people can't." Some who ventured up the Mormon Road into the San Bernardino Mountains saw gold to be extracted from Bear Valley mines. To others, green forests took on the appearance of evergreen emeralds waiting to be cut, hauled away, and sold. Dr. David Noble Smith, builder of the first road into Arrowhead Mountain's active thermal hot springs area saw this unique high country as a life-enhancing environment where one could refresh both body and soul.

Smith constructed a small building called Dr. D.N. Smith's Hygienic Infirmary. He and his paying guests/patients touted the curative powers of the hot springs, mud and mineral baths, and even that of the nearby cold springs. In the 1870s, Smith enlarged his "health club" to include several private rooms. These ultimately were replaced with a 40-room, 3-story Arrowhead Springs Hotel. Adding to the drama and flavor of the resort's location was the 7-1/2-acre natural Arrowhead formation for which the mountain itself had been named, easily visible from the hotel grounds. During its heyday the spa and hotel were served by Pacific Electric Red Cars which sometimes made five round-trips daily to the resort from metropolitan Los Angeles.

Arrowhead Springs was not the only hot springs thought to provide curative powers. Crafton's Retreat in the eastern end of the valley also grew in fame as a health-related resort during the 1870s. The popularity of Arrowhead Springs continues to the present day as bottled water

from these same mountain springs is sold throughout California.

To Little Bear Valley's Frank Talmadge Arrowhead water was not only good for drinking. He was the first to build a water-powered sawmill in Little Bear Valley. The Talmadge name frequently dots historical records of Little Bear and Huston Flats (present day Lake Gregory). Versatile and highly talented, Talmadge is remembered for having been a cattle rancher, timber baron, gold prospector, and community leader. Like several men who considered the mountain country their permanent home, and not merely a land to exploit, Talmadge was interested in the future of the area. And that future was fast approaching.

Rapid expansion of the railroad soon linked Southern California with the rest of the nation. By 1873 two transcontinental systems—the Southern Pacific and the Santa Fe—hitched Los Angeles with points East. Big rolling engines and high pitched steam whistles replaced much of the stage traffic leading into Southern California. Citrus harvests increased steadily, led largely by the growing popularity of the valley's sweet, seedless oranges. The more that visitors heralded the healthful environment of the local mountains, and valleys, the more others came to see for themselves. Many who came decided to stay.

At the foot of the mountains, Frank E. Brown and Edward G. Judson developed a planned community. They called it Redlands after the terra-cotta color of the rich soil. Natural promoters, the two men publicized the new area using a picture-filled map of Redlands showing street names which had not yet even been surveyed. The only real obstacle standing between the developers and the fulfillment of their dreams was an adequate water supply for the fledgling community. Dr. Benjamin Barton, a state assemblyman and pioneering physician, no doubt was influential in bringing the state engineer to Bear Valley to consider the site as a possible reservoir. The valley was said to afford an ideal spot for a dam.

Brown wasted no time in organizing Bear Valley Land and Water Company. Construction of the dam began in the summer of 1884. A Yale graduate with an engineering degree, Brown put his schooling to the ultimate test by designing a granite, single arch, ashlar rock dam using cement brought in from Great Britain. His original design called for a dam that was 53 feet high, 335 feet across, with a 20-foot wide spillway 4 feet lower than the top. Because the structure could not impound enough water to meet its obligations, in 1910 a new dam was built which measured 72

CALIFORNIA BLACK OAK

A SPECTACULAR DECIDUOUS OAK IT UNDOUBTEDLY DERIVED ITS NAME BECAUSE OF ITS VERY DARK-COLORED BARK. LEAVES WHEN FIRST APPEARING ON YOUNG SHOOTS IN THE EARLY SPRING MAY BE BRIGHT GREEN AS THEY MATURE AND USUALLY TURN YELLOW TO REDDISH IN THE FALL, PRODUCING AN INTERESTING COLOR EFFECT ON THE CALIFORNIA FOOTHILLS AND MOUNTAINS. AT LOWER ELEVATIONS IT IS A GRACEFUL TREE WITH A BROAD, ROUNDED CROWN WHILE AT HIGHER ELEVATIONS IT TENDS TO BE SOMEWHAT MORE IRREGULARLY BRANCHED AND MAY, ON OCCASION, DEVELOP AN ALMOST PROSTRATE FORM.

feet in height. As a result of this bold engineering feat, what was then the world's largest man-made lake had been created. In the century it has been in operation, it has withstood earthquakes, floods, and drastic temperature ranges which have varied from 30 degrees below zero to 100 degrees above. Its designer/builder was proudly honored by his alma mater, and the community of Redlands was blessed with an abundant and much needed source of water to fuel its rapid growth.

The entire San Bernardino Valley was subsequently developed as the citrus producing capital of the world. Oranges dominated the list followed by lemons and grapefruit. Up in the mountains, the harvest continued to be that of the forest itself as unchecked logging activities continued to strip the high country bare.

In 1884, Gus Knight Junior established Pine Knot Lodge

on the shores of the newly created mountain lake, thus inaugurating Bear Valley's destiny as an international mountain resort. Of the ten baronial estates existing in Bear Valley at the time, all were subsequently subdivided and transformed, with the building of stately Normandy homes, or Nordic, or Swiss, or ranch houses and the establishment of numerous lakeside lodges. Sportsmen quickly discovered the glistening lake, beautiful vistas, plentiful fish, and peaceful resorts.

William Talmadge, Frank's son, not one to let an opportunity pass him by, built a new sawmill on the edge of the lake where he began harvesting the flooded trees. No doubt Talmadge wondered about the future of his own little valley – Little Bear Valley – and no doubt the idea of another reservoir had crossed his mind. It was definitely on the minds of a lot of other people.

GREY SQUIRREL

A MAN KNOWN AS "DAD" SKINNER IS REGARDED AS THE FIRST ONE-MAN CHAMBER OF COMMERCE FOR THE BIG BEAR AREA. IN A 1922 BIG BEAR LAKE CHAMBER OF COMMERCE *MOTORLOGUE* ARTICLE, DAD SKINNER WROTE:

THERE'S AN INVISIBLE SIGN OVER EVERY ROAD LEADING INTO THIS MAGICAL PINE-CLAD, FERNFRINGED FOREST SURROUNDING THE WONDER LAKE OF THE HIGHLANDS—A SIGN AND A COMMAND, "LEAVE CARE BEHIND ALL YE WHO ENTER HERE!" AND, WHETHER ONE WILLS IT OR NOT, THE BURDEN OF WORRY, THE PALL OF TROUBLE, THE WEIGHT OF RESPONSIBILITY YOU HAVE CARRIED TIL IT SEEMS AN INSEPARABLE PART OF YOUR BEING, IMPERCEPTIBLY LIGHTENS AND LIFTS AND DRIFTS AWAY TO THE DISTANT MOUNTAIN TOPS AT THE SILENT BIDDING OF MOTHER NATURE AND BIG BEAR LAKE.

At the turn of the century those who lived and worked in the San Bernardino Mountains were eager to end their isolation. Meanwhile, "flatlanders" in the valley were thirsty for more irrigation water. Planning for both a new highway and another major reservoir to meet all of these needs occurred simultaneously. In 1891, an engineer named Adolph Koebig was hired by the newly incorporated Arrowhead Reservoir Company to complete surveys at three potential reservoir sites, all of which ultimately became lakes—Grass Valley (Grass Valley Lake), Little Bear Valley (Lake Arrowhead), and Huston Flats (Lake Gregory).

James Gamble, president of Proctor and Gamble and chief financier behind the newly incorporated reservoir company, cast the deciding vote in favor of Little Bear Valley.

Before long, San Bernardino was buzzing with enthusiasm over news that a forthcoming highway and irrigation project at Little Bear Creek would rival Redland's Bear Valley Dam. Southern Californians envisioned journeying up to mountain resorts on a wide, smooth road. Soon, both logging and road building crews swung into action.

Completed one year later, the new Arrowhead Reservoir Road reduced the average grade of the steep mountain ascent to eight percent. Starting just above Arrowhead Hot Springs and running up Waterman Canyon, then east across the mountain to Little Bear Valley, this highway was a vast improvement over the Old Mormon logging road.

Other changes took place while work crews made painstaking progress on the reservoir itself. A group of business men bought a Grass Valley sawmill, formed the Arrowhead Mountain Club, and opened a lodge above the horseshoe bend (today's Arrowhead Highlands) in the new road. Named after the title of author Frank Stockton's book, *Squirrel Inn*, the rustic lodge included individual cottages. It quickly grew in popularity among Arrowhead Reservoir Company management and other influential citizens of the day.

Unnoticed by all but the most perceptive it was literally the establishment of this particular lodge that formed the catalyst for turning back the loggers and the trend towards exploitation. During the decades that followed emphasis would shift almost imperceptibly towards a desire to perserve and restore a natural resource whose value

had only begun to be appreciated. A revolutionary concept, this trend toward conservation, it was nurtured within the walls of Squirrel Inn as men of power and influence pondered Arrowhead Mountain's vulnerability. How long before the alpine beauty that surrounded them would itself be felled by the axe or at the hands of engineering crews?

Firm action needed to be taken to prevent such a treasure from being wiped out. In 1893, President Benjamin Harrison, at the insistance of men who had been at Squirrel Inn, set aside 737,280 acres of land in the San Bernardino Mountains as a national forest reserve. Adolph Koebig, overseer of the Arrowhead Reservoir Company, in particular had insisted this conservation effort be mounted. A portrait of President Harrison was hung in the Squirrel Inn Lodge in response to the Chief Executive's bold action.

As the twentieth century dawned, work on the reservoir at Little Bear Valley (soon renamed Lake Arrowhead) was well underway. In April, 1905, Little Bear Dam stood an imposing 43 feet high. The spacious meadowlands of this high country valley, together with the remnants of the Talmadge and LaPraix sawmills, were rapidly vanishing under watershed impounded by the wall, marking the end of an era. From obscurity Arrowhead was about to be thrust into the limelight of world fame. As the project neared completion, the Arrowhead Reservoir Company changed its name to Arrowhead Reservoir and Power Company and announced plans to build a "mammoth hotel" in Little Bear that would rival any such establishment in the world. This lodge would boast cottages, an amusement arcade, and a lake stocked with trout. The company also admitted it had plans to supply water and hydraulic power not only to San Bernardino, as originally intended, but also to Victor Valley and the Mojave Desert.

In May, 1908, Arrowhead Reservoir Company sent 17 wagons pulled by six- and eight-horse teams to participate in an industrial parade as part of San Bernardino's Festival of the Arrowhead. Later that summer, the Outlet Tower at the portal of Tunnel #1 was completed connecting the watershed of Little Bear Valley with that of Grass Valley and signaling that the project was near its end. After 15 years of work, the reservoir was nearly ready to be filled, its water to be sent rushing down into the thirsty valley. Then, as with the Mormons before them, the winds of change threatened the entire enterprise and it suddenly became doubtful whether

"A FOREST IS A THING OF INFINITE MYSTERY, OF MULTIPLE DETAIL, OF IMMEASURABLE DESIGN . . . IF THE FORESTS PERISHED, THERE WOULD BE LEFT ONLY DESERT, DESOLATE AND DEAD."
—ZANE GREY

BERT SWITZER
THE MOUNTAIN'S FIRST RANGER

IN, 1900, A GAUNT YOUNG MAN INFECTED WITH TUBERCULOSIS (THE LEADING CAUSE OF DEATH IN THOSE DAYS) WAS, WITH HIS WIFE SARA, AMONG A MULTITUDE OF CAMPERS AT RUNNING SPRINGS. WITH HIS WIFE'S HELP AND THE FRESH, DRY AIR OF THE HIGH COUNTRY, SWITZER RECOVERED AND BECAME THE MOUNTAIN'S FIRST U.S. FOREST RANGER, SERVING UNTIL 1923.

or not the huge irrigation project would ever come to fruition.

In a Kern River case that became known as the Miller-Lux decision of 1908, the California courts prohibited transferring water from one watershed to another. This decision seemed on face value to rule out the possibility that Little Bear Reservoir water would ever be used to irrigate San Bernardino as such water flowed naturally north into the desert, not south towards the coast. And so after withstanding fires, floods and obstacles of every kind, the project's ultimate fate stood in the balance, waiting to be determined by a court of law.

The Arrowhead Reservoir and Power Company, believing its appeal would be successful, proceeded to complete the reservoir. In 1913, they even sought permission to issue $4 million in bonds to finance completion of the work. The Railroad Commission which governed the matter turned down the bond issue "until title for the water can be determined in court." When that title was finally determined, the Arrowhead Reservoir and Power Company was enjoined against tunneling water for irrigation into the San Bernardino Valley. Thus, after an effort that lasted more than two decades, the project was doomed. Yet as fate would have it, this failed irrigation project gave birth to what would become Southern California's most beautiful mountain resort—Lake Arrowhead.

To most people who delighted in the mountains for their pine scented forests and stark, rugged beauty, legal battles were of little concern. As long as squirrels darted in the trees overhead or nibbled food from their fingertips; as long as an evening walk produced numerous deer sightings; as long as trips out on Big Bear Lake produced a good catch of trout, the resorts would prosper in spite of long-winded lawyers who argued over the future of the area.

Turning its attention from irrigation to recreation, Arrowhead Reservoir and Power Company denied a local group of sportsmen calling themselves the Little Bear Association, from fishing in the new lake, even though the Association volunteered to stock it themselves. Company officials said fishing would become the exclusive privilege of visitors at the proposed new resort.

With or without an invitation, 1915 saw the first wooden boat launched on Little Bear Lake. Soon thereafter, hundreds of anglers converged on the lake and its surrounding streams. Each drew full limits of trout on opening day, April 3. Four days later, Mr. Victor Smith of the Company declared the lake closed to the public. The outcry was so loud that County Supervisors were asked to arbitrate. Not knowing which way to turn, the Supervisors instead focused on efforts to improve the quality and quantity of roads leading into the south side of Big Bear Lake where there were no fishing related disputes.

In fact, it was a major new road—a 101-mile long "Rim of the World Drive"—that dominated the news of the day. In its early days, this scenic road was among the most publicized highways in the West. Credit for its inception goes to Dr. John Baylis of San Bernardino who envisioned a continuous loop around the mountain communities. Two years in the making, it was dedicated in July of 1916 with much pomp and circumstance.

SAN GORGONIO WILDERNESS

rimeval and aloof, the isolated, soaring rampart that constitutes Mt. San Jacinto (Saint Hyacinth) stood nonetheless vulnerable to the loggers as well. All but forgotten, so precipitous and foreboding was the 10,786 foot massif, even the Cahuilla Indians regarded this somber granite mountain as a dwelling place of angry gods not to be trespassed against.

It was from the less perpendicular southwest slope that Paul Bunyan came. By the early 1890s these once silent woods resounded with the thunder of falling trees. Acre by acre, timber barons like Amasa Saunders hacked away at the virgin mountain forest, cutting ever farther up the western slopes of Mt. San Jacinto. Behind them came sheep and cattle by the thousands, herded to summer pastures in the high-country meadows along newly opened logging roads.

In 1897 a bill was signed by President Grover Cleveland creating the San Jacinto Forest Reserve. A reserve in name only however, as was the case in the San Bernardinos, most mountainlands remained in private hands.

RACCOON

1898 saw the arrival of the nation's first forest rangers. Zealously guarding as best they could what little remained pristine in Southern California's mountain country, forestry personnel chased cattlemen and shepherds out of the highlands, put a stop to logging on public lands, and valiantly fought off numerous outbreaks of forest fires.

Too little, too late, it was only after all but the most inaccessible old-growth woods had been plundered that the logging operations moved on. Nevertheless, from such chaotic beginnings, the United States Forest Service as we know it today was born.

With no large lakes such as those now to be found at Little Bear and Big Bear Valley, Mt. San Jacinto remained largely overlooked by the growing tourism industry. A world-famed sanitarium, later replaced by the Idyllwild Inn, brought the area some notoriety. In and around the mill sites of Strawberry Valley, on the western slope of San Jacinto, grew the town of Idyllwild, while the forest took to healing itself under the ever watchful eye of the United States Forest Service.

"THE VIEW FROM SAN JACINTO IS THE MOST SUBLIME SPECTACLE TO BE FOUND ANYWHERE ON THIS EARTH."

—JOHN MUIR

old had brought about the birth of Big Bear. Logging of the high country plateau that is Arrowhead Mountain initiated settlement of Little Bear. While fledgling resorts inaugurated what would, a half century later, become a multimillion dollar tourist industry, still a handfull of die-hard gold-seekers continued to scour the range and one man in particular, Mr. J.E. Brookings, persisted in extracting a fortune from that which remained of Arrowhead's forest primeval.

During his boyhood, Brookings witnessed the logging off of Michigan's old-growth white pine forest. Growing up amidst lumberjacks of the Northwoods it was a trade he felt well prepared for. What with timber reserves all but exhausted in the East, Brookings set his sights on California where, in 1899, he purchased the Highland Lumber Company Mill near what is now the town of Running Springs.

Together with his son and cousin, Brookings established the most dynamic logging operation in the history of the Southwest. Camps were established throughout the back country, all connected by a narrow gauge rail line. A state-of-the-art mill was built at Fredalba, near Running Springs. So efficient were the logging methods of the Brookings Mill that before long the most impressive forest titans on the mountain had been laid to waste.

Alarmed at what was happening, concerned local citizens petitioned President Theodore Roosevelt to expand upon Harrison's forest reserve to encompass and thus rescue all remaining privately held timberland in the San Bernardino Mountains. The year was 1906. An enormous demand for orange crates kept the Brookings Mill operating day and night. With 100 million board feet of virgin timber on his land and the precision of three steam locomotives, hard working loggers and the largest sawmill operation in the Southwest, Brookings proceeded literally to strip the mountain bare.

Long before legislation could be enacted, the damage had been done. Green Valley and environs stood completely denuded. Brookings moved on to the town that today bares his name in Oregon where he invested his fortunes into even grander logging operations, selling out the lands he had laid to waste in Southern California to resort developers.

A prolific second generation forest has since reclaimed much of what looked at the time like a war zone. Fires have twice burned through much of the Brookings land holdings, however, leaving today's Heaps Peak and environs noticeably void of forest. Purists among today's mountaineers seek out isolated recesses of this bridge between the highlands of Arrowhead and alpine Big Bear where grand old-growth forest monarchs still stand, spared Brookings efficiency due to the difficulty of the rugged terrain that they dominate.

BIG CONE SPRUCE

A SUBSPECIES OF THE DOUGLAS FIR OCCURING ONLY IN SOUTHERN CALIFORNIA, BIG CONE SPRUCE IS ALSO OFTEN REFERRED TO AS FALSE HEMLOCK. CONTEMPORARY TO THE ANCIENT FORESTS OF REDWOODS THAT ONCE THRIVED AS FAR SOUTH AS LOS ANGELES, THIS BEAUTIOUS CONIFER LOOKS TRADITIONAL ENOUGH WITH ITS YOUTHFUL, CONICAL SHAPE. AS IT MATURES, HOWEVER, IT ASSUMES A MOST PREHISTORIC-LOOKING PROFILE. UNGAINLY UPPER LIMBS STRETCH OFF ENDLESSLY IN ALL DIRECTIONS GIVING IT THE APPEARANCE OF SOMETHING FROM THE AGE OF DINOSAURS. A TAP ROOT OF INCREDIBLE DEPTH ALLOWS IT TO ESTABLISH ITSELF AT ELEVATIONS OF AS LOW AS 2,000 FEET WHERE, IN COOL, SHADED RECESSES IT WITHSTANDS THE ANNUAL DROUGHT THAT HOLDS BACK THE ADVANCE OF ITS HIGH-COUNTRY COMRADES.

RANGE: THROUGHOUT THE MOUNTAINS OF SOUTHERN CALIFORNIA FROM ELEVATIONS OF 6,000 TO 2,000 FEET.

ALPINE PARADISE

IN THE EARLY PART OF THE 20TH CENTURY, RECORDING ARTIST FRANK SILVERWOOD CUT AN EDISON RECORD THAT SUMMED UP A LOT OF PEOPLE'S FEELINGS FOR THE MOUNTAIN RESORTS.

"WHERE THE SNOW-CROWNED
GOLDEN SIERRA
KEEP THEIR WATCH O'ER THE
VALLEY'S BLOOM
IT IS THERE I WOULD BE
IN OUR LAND BY THE SEA
EVERY BREEZE BEARING
RICH PERFUME.

"IT IS HERE NATURE GIVES
OF HER RAREST
IT IS HOME, SWEET HOME TO
ME
AND I KNOW WHEN I DIE
I SHALL BREATHE MY LAST
SIGH
FOR MY SUNNY
CALIFORNIA."

ith the 1916 completion of Rim of the World Drive, the gates to an Alpine Paradise were flung wide open. Tourism took off as did a variety of other new enterprises, as everything from moonshine stills and speakeasys to silver fox farms and plush dinner houses flourished in these now accessible woods.

Americans were in love with their automobiles. For Southern Californians, the increased mobility meant frequent weekend trips and vacations to a certain towering Alpine mountain range with its beautiful mile-high lakes.

Hollywood filmmakers wasted no time in utilizing the now readily available backgrounds of Little Bear Lake and Big Bear Lake in their motion pictures. One of the earliest records of location filming in the area dates back to 1911 when G.M. Anderson of Santa Monica shot a western called *The Romance of the Bar O* along the headwaters of the Santa Ana River. Anderson had hardly pulled out when the Bison Motion Picture Company of New Jersey arrived with a company of about 100 for a production featuring Bear Valley Dam in the background. Bison continued work on other productions including several westerns. More movie companies followed including both Fox and Universal.

In 1914, two of Hollywood's premier directors shot pictures in the mountains. Cecil B. deMille made *Call of the North* in Bear Valley while D.W. Griffith used the locale in producing *Clansman* later released as the epic *Birth of a Nation*. Another company filmed a story called *Mona the Mountain Maid* based on a popular mountain activity of the day—making moonshine. The film starred Mona Darkfeather, an Indian Princess. So realistic was the distillery used in making the picture that federal agents actually raided the movie set .

Mountain lodges, restaurants, and supply stores catered to the moviemakers and the tourists who came up to fish, hunt, swim, or just relax. Cross-country skiing became tremendously popular in the 1920s. Big Bear, Little Bear, and the surrounding communities of Crestline, Blue Jay, and Big Pines became popular winter sport areas, as logging operations shut down and outdoor recreational facilities flourished.

In spite of the transformation which was underway, Arrowhead Reservoir and Power Company directors nevertheless tired of the burdens, risks, responsibilities, and high costs of owning and managing their fledgling resort. In a fairly sudden move, a group of 10 Los Angeles businessmen formed Arrowhead Lake Company in 1921 and purchased all properties and assets of the Arrowhead Reservoir and Power Company, together with its now 47,000 acre-

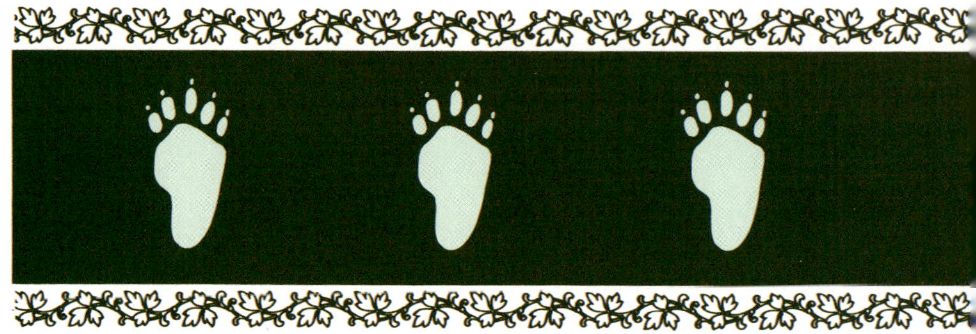

feet of water. One of the new principals, A.E. Warmington, announced that henceforth Little Bear Lake would be known as *Lake Arrowhead.* He also announced that he and his partners intended to spend millions on roads, new lodges, a pavilion, boat houses, a luxury hotel, an ice plant, fish hatchery, golf course, and shops for merchants.

Arrowhead Lake Company wasted no time in putting their plan into action. Backed by an $8,000 per day payroll, the company built eight camps in the valley which could accommodate 600 laborers. Work commenced on the construction of a uniquely styled Norman Village, a grand pavilion, and an "olde English clubhouse" on the north shore. During its official opening on July 24, 1922, the Arrowhead Lake Company hosted 250 newspapermen and women to a day of feasting, fishing, boating, swimming, dancing and tours of the new Arrowhead Lodge, Village Inn and North Shore Tavern. Rave reviews were voiced by all in attendance. At last the vision of a resort to rival Europe's finest had been realized.

Neighbors in Big Bear Valley were enjoying quite a summer themselves. Forty-four resorts were in full operation. All were supplied for the first time that year with electricity. More than 10,000 cars poured into the City of Big Bear Lake on July 4. The distinctly western-style Bear Valley Country Club staged a pit buffalo meat barbecue, while over a thousand people attended a July 20 barn dance at the newly constructed Big Bear Pavilion.

By the summer of 1928, Arrowhead Lake Company had launched a major marketing effort. Calling Arrowhead "California's finest playground," the company placed a full page advertisement in the *Los Angeles Times* boasting "exhilarating air, dancing every night," and rowing, boating, fishing for rainbow trout, hunting, bathing (swimming), horseback riding, and golf. Lots at Lake Arrowhead in Arrowhead Woods sold for between $650 and $15,000 with 25 percent down and a minimum of $10 per month payment at an interest rate of seven percent. Average cost to build per square foot was listed at $3 and up. Urbanization of the forest began in earnest as successful Southern California professionals and Hollywood moguls built charming homes and magnificent estates throughout both alpine Arrowhead and Big Bear.

When the Great Depression of the 1930s hit the Alps of Southern California, its effect was not nearly as devastating as in other parts of the country. While it managed to slow down development and the tourism that fueled such growth, it failed to bring a halt to expansionism. Arrowhead had become well established as a Hollywood retreat.

LAKE ARROWHEAD VILLAGE

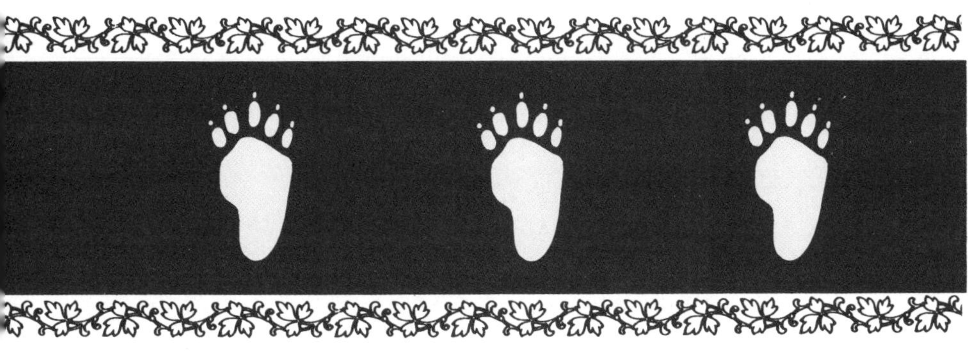

THE STORY OF ARROWHEAD SPRINGS

Perhaps more than any one person in the history of the San Bernardino Mountains, the name *Dr. David Noble Smith* should stand as the individual most responsible for broadcasting the magic, the mystique, the romance, and the wonder that is associated with this area. It was Smith who in 1857 built the first permanent structure at Arrowhead Springs to promote the hot springs as a place of beauty where life could be restored and rejuvenated. Destitute when he first reached his hand into the warm waters below the great Arrowhead on the mountainside, David Noble Smith had tried prospecting but to no avail. Originally from Ohio, he wandered through parts of Texas and Illinois in search of something. He didn't know exactly what. He remarked that he felt "like a wanderer in search of a lost home."

Smith was a medical doctor by training and longed to aid in the war against tuberculosis but as of yet, he hadn't come upon a way he felt he could seriously contribute. At his father's deathbed, Smith reported a strange and unusual experience. He said he felt he "was taken" by what he thought was a "saint" to a spot where a unique combination of climate and curative waters "fused in such a manner so as to perform miraculous cures for all lung diseases." As if that wasn't dramatic enough, Smith claimed that the spot was marked by a "gigantic Arrowhead." When he first set eyes on the Arrowhead of the San Bernardinos, Smith knew he was "home" at last.

By 1863, Dr. Smith had earned enough capital to begin his project and on April 14, 1864 newspaper articles reported that the Hot Springs Infirmary was open to the public.

Two rough decades followed. Dr. Smith's first wife, a patient at the infirmary who had been abandoned by her former husband, died. With his second wife, Smith had three children, one of whom died at 3 years of age and another at 17. Some attributed the deaths of otherwise healthy patients to Smith, citing his curious methods of treatment. His own 17-year-old daughter is thought to have died of complications resulting from Smith requiring her to immerse herself in icy spring waters.

Through storms of controversy Smith never lost his personal vision of the power of the springs. But financial difficulties, an increasingly wary public, and his own personal problems forced Smith to give up the springs around 1884. Subsequent proprietors developed the area as a resort which, during Hollywood's Golden Era, attracted the investment dollars of film mogul Darryl Zanuck and screen star Claudette Colbert.

THE SKYLAND INN WAS A POPULAR SPOT AMONG MOTION PICUTRE PRODUCTION COMPANIES. IT IS REMEMBERED FOR ITS PLAYER PIANO, STORY HOURS FOR CHILDREN, AND ENTERTAINING ATMOSPHERE. ON ONE FESTIVE OCCASION, EVERYBODY WAS HEARD SINGING A UNIQUE MOUNTAIN VERSION OF *TRAIL OF THE LONESOME PINE.*

"IN THE GRAND OLD SAN
BERNARDINOMOUNTAINS
I WILL MEET YOU IN
THOUSAND PINES
WHERE THE BREEZES SIGH
THROUGH THE PINE TREES
HIGH
THERE LET ME LIVE AND LET
ME DIE
OH JUNE AND JULY ARE
DIVINE!
AUGUST, TOO, AND
SEPTEMBER ARE FINE
IN THE GRAND OLD SAN
BERNARDINO MOUNTAINS
I'LL MEET YOU AT
THOUSAND PINES."

As long as the dream factories were in production, the mountain resorts thrived.

Charles S. Mann and H.W. Ramsey proceeded with their plans of developing the former Mormon Springs area (present day Crestline) with zeal. At the same time, they continued promoting other high country communities including Arrowhead Woods, Strawberry Flats, Cedar Pines Park, and Skyland. Together they built roads, installed water and power lines, and thus inaugurated the urbanization of the high country.

Camp Seeley, at today's Cedar Pines Park, was another popular year 'round resort of the day which like so many of the mountain communities had once been a small logging camp. Seeley offered visitors sledding, tobogganing, and snow skiing in the winter months. The California Ski Championships were held there in 1931.

The first ski jump in the mountains was built in 1929 at Big Pines near Wrightwood, where, a world ski jumping record was set. Similar big jumps were later constructed at Big Bear and near Running Springs.

In 1934, Arthur Gregory, a major mountain land owner, marshalled support for the 50-year-old idea of creating a lake in Huston Flats. Through his efforts, a 75-foot-high dam was constructed on Huston Creek in 1938. Lake Gregory was born. Today Lake Gregory Regional Park with its attendant Village is a popular recreational spot in the San Bernardino Mountains.

Downhill skiing continued to grow in popularity. In addition to the creation of Lake Gregory by Redlands developer Arthur Gregory, 1934 also saw the construction of a sling lift at Fish Camp (present day Snow Valley). Soon an additional lift was added at Big Bear in 1938. The first chairlift was installed at Snow Valley in 1948.

In the 1930s and early 1940s Lake Arrowhead continued to cash in on its long-standing relationship with Hollywood. Some of the film industry's biggest stars—Charlie Chaplin, Bing Crosby, Jane Wyman, Clark Gable, Marlene Dietrich, Myrna Loy, and Claudette Colbert were frequent guests at the lodge while many film personalities maintained homes around the lake.

This was also the era of the Big Bands. On summer nights, swing music swept across the lake from the village pavilion, filling Little Bear Valley with the most popular tunes of the day. Although the Hollywood connection helped define Arrowhead's image as an Alpine Paradise, it was World War II and not the Depression that caused a drop in mountain tourism. Rumors that the resort was up for sale appeared in local tabloids.

Trying to run the entire resort operations indeed had

"THE SNOW-CROWNED MONARCHS THAT HAVE AS A FOOTSTOOL SAN BERNARDINO'S VALLEY OF ROMANCE RANK AMONG THE GREATEST MOUNTAINS OF THE WORLD, TITANIC, TEN THOUSAND FOOT PYRAMIDS, PRIMEVAL, SUBLIME, EVERLASTING."
— DR. GILBERT ELLIS BAILEY, UNIVERSITY OF SOUTHERN CALIFORNIA

proven too much for the Arrowhead Lake Company. In the wake of World War II, the company declared bankruptcy. The year was 1946. Dr. Charles Strub of the Los Angeles Turf Club and owner of the Santa Anita race track acquired the lake and surrounding property for a mere $2 million. Strub, a resident of Lake Arrowhead, thought the best way to run the resort would be to lease out the different businesses, which he proceeded to do successfully. Commerce in the village picked up and the 1950s and 1960s proved to be prosperous years.

Still another new lake and recreational playground was born in the San Bernardino Mountains. Planned as part of the California Water Project of the 1960s, Lake Silverwood was created as a water storage reservoir where the former village of Cedar Springs had stood. Lake Silverwood dam today stretches more than 200 feet across the west fork of the Mojave River. Silverwood has become popular for its excellent campgrounds and public marina.

In 1960 after the death of Dr. Strub, a businessman named Jules Berman, owner of Kahlua coffee liqueur, together with two other investors bought the Lake Arrowhead resort. Berman implemented a workable plan to subdivide Lake Arrowhead properties, thus instigating the true urbanization of Arrowhead Woods. Berman also built a beautiful new country club and 18-hole golf course in Grass Valley. In 1967, Berman's lake and village assets were merged with those of the huge Boise Cascade corporation.

Subsequently, Boise Cascade sold the country club and golf course to California Golf and Tennis. In 1975, both the lake and golf course were subsequently sold to an association of residents which today owns the properties around the lake. Boise Cascade retained ownership of the village until 1977 when it sold the land and buildings to a former executive with the company who had formed Metropolitan Advertising Company. In 1978, Metropolitan sold the village to developer George Coult, president of GC Properties in Irvine, California.

The decade between 1968 and 1978 took its toll on the village and its buildings. With ownership changing hands so often, the Tyrolean structures had gradually slipped into distress. Coult determined that the best way to improve the place was to start all over again. He put the torch to the village, burning it to the ground in 1979. He then completely rebuilt the entire resort to its present day status. Today, a virtual Disneyland in the woods, Lake Arrowhead Village is a world-class resort.

Meanwhile ownership of water rights at Big Bear Lake had resulted in heated controversies. Since the creation of

BLUE JAY VILLAGE

"THESE MOUNTAINS HAVE BEEN MANY THINGS TO MANY MEN, BUT NONE HAVE SEEN THEM WHOLE. LIKE ALL GREAT MYSTERIES THEY ARE GREATER THAN THE SUM OF THEIR PARTS, AND FAMILIARITY BUT DEFINES BETTER THE TERMS OF THEIR ENIGMA." – FRANK WATERS

Bear Valley Lake and up until the late 1970s, water rights and adjacent property were owned by Bear Valley Mutual Water Company and its forerunner companies. The lake lived up to its original purpose of supplying water to Redlands. In doing so, water needs weren't always met at the constantly growing mountain lake resort. Too often, Big Bear Municipal Water District had to contend with severely fluctuating water levels which threatened the resort potential of the entire area.

In 1966, the water company formed Bear Valley Development Company for the purpose of selling lake property. This meant even more people would be building homes on the lake thus placing even greater demands on constant high levels of water for recreational purposes.

In 1975, Big Bear Municipal Water District filed a suit against Bear Valley Mutual Water Company. In a 1977 court decision, Big Bear Municipal Water District paid $4.7 million for 3,006 acres below the high water level, the two dams and rights to all natural inflow. This clearly shifted the role of Big Bear Lake from that of a major water supplier to Redlands and confirmed its role as one of Southern California's major resort areas. As a result of the change, property values soared and the Big Bear Water District was charged with the task of maintaining dams and water levels. Under this arrangement which has worked successfully for the past decade, Big Bear Lake and the cities of Big Bear, Big Bear Lake, and Fawnskin have thrived.

Today, the community is looking forward to the construction of a new Big Bear Dam which, like the original, will be a model of state-of-the-art water reclamation engineering.

CHIPMUNK

Alpenguide

Towering above Los Angeles from Malibu to Palm Springs, the Alps of Southern California create a dramatic backdrop for a dynamic city. To the casual observer looking up from the base of these stone ramparts, the impression given is one of a somewhat barren and austere environment. Much to the explorer's delight and surprise, however, a trip above the 4,000-foot level leads you into a fabulous timber belt of aromatic pine and cedar, flowering dogwood, cascading streams, and clear, high-country lakes. In a matter of moments one experiences the sensation of having been transported from Southern California to Bavaria. Such is the natural beauty and spectacular panoramas afforded to those who venture up into the mountains.

FORESTS OFFER QUIET, A CHANCE FOR SOLITUDE AND INTROSPECTION. IT IS LITTLE WONDER THEN THAT THESE FORESTS HOST MILLIONS OF VISITORS EACH YEAR.

More accessible than any other range in the State, excellent highways traverse the lowlands, skirt the canyons, and carry the traveler swiftly soaring into tall timber. Plan to travel during the early morning and early evening hours, when landscapes appear most dramatic and wildlife is active. Spend mid-day shopping or playing in any one of the many resort destinations found here. Temperatures tend to average 20 degrees below that of the surrounding lowlands, so carry a jacket or sweater with you during even the warmest of weather.

ROY MURPHY

The Alps of Southern California are alive with colorful flora and fauna. Stellar jays (above) enliven even the deepest thicket with their endless chattering. The brilliant Western Tanager (opposite page, upper right) adds a splash of color against the somber evergreens. Playful gray squirrels (right) are ever present, darting from forest floor to treetop and back again.

Pinecones of every shape and size abound as do, in season, the beautiful white blossoms of the Pacific Coast Dogwood (far right).

MAZIE HOLES

JAN WASSINK

ROY MURPHY

ROY MURPHY

ROY MURPHY

DAVE DELILLE

DAVE DELILLE

LAKE ARROWHEAD VILLAGE (above and left) recreates tyrolean charm amidst this uniquely alpine, yet Southern Californian environment. Among the more beautiful year-round residents of this mountain community is the colorful wood duck (far left).

GRAY SQUIRREL
AND CHICKADEE

FINE CRAFTED
FURNISHINGS AT
LAKE ARROWHEAD'S
"MOUNTAIN HAUS
INTERIORS"

Leaving behind the bucolic Southern California of popular notion, you will enter either the San Bernardino or Angeles National Forests. Within their boundaries are more than 20 campgrounds and eight government-designated wilderness areas. Awe-inspiring landscapes reveal themselves at every turn of the mountain road, particularly on clear days when one can see from alpine meadows across the Los Angeles basin to the sparkling waters of the Pacific Ocean.

The 101-mile long Rim of the World Drive (State Highway 18) is the most popular of these routes. Ascending the perpendicular southern slope of Arrowhead Mountain it only skirts the true high country, however, without actually penetrating the woodlands. To discover the beauty of the forest, meadows, lakes, and villages, leave the highway at any of a dozen turnoffs and explore.

Stop first at Lake Arrowhead, the Bavarian-style village with a history as exciting and colorful as the movie moguls who inspired its conception. Architectural design blended with scenic natural surroundings are what one might expect to find in southern Switzerland. Socially exclusive, Arrowhead, with its spectacular lakeside estates and charming mountain homes, is truly the crown jewel of Southern California's Alps. A turn of the forest road (State Highway 173) leads you to an alpine village that seems to rise out of a blue mirror lake. Lake Arrowhead and its village have been performing magic on the unsuspecting traveler for years. More than half a century ago this setting enchanted Shirley Temple when Little Bear Valley doubled for Switzerland during the filming of *Heidi*.

In Lake Arrowhead Village numerous boutiques, shops, galleries, and fine restaurants provide for hours of entertainment. Water sports are in order as is a relaxing nap lakeside on the beach. For those curious about the famous celebrities who have made Arrowhead the mountain playground that it is, a boat tour on the *Arrowhead Queen* (a 60-passenger paddlewheeler) is highly recommended and thoroughly entertaining.

Consisting of 786 surface acres and 14 miles of shoreline, Lake Arrowhead is nothing less than spectacular and breathtaking. Launching of boats on this privately owned lake is limited to local property owners. Boat rentals are available to the public, however, at the South Shore Marina.

From sleeping out under the stars to lodging in a world-class resort hotel, a night out in Lake Arrowhead is guaranteed to be a memorable experience. Although numerous camping facilities are to be found throughout Southern

California's high country, Lake Arrowhead's Dogwood Campground is by far and away one of the finest mountain campgrounds in the entire U.S. Forest Service system. Nature trails, campfire programs and beautiful campsites set deep in the forest are certain to make of any visitor one happy camper. For those less inclined to roughing it, Lake Arrowhead Hilton Lodge offers the ultimate in comfort and casual elegance. Historic Saddleback Inn as well as other hostelries are also available for guests at Lake Arrowhead Village.

Neighboring Blue Jay, considered the gateway to Lake Arrowhead, sports a Bavarian motif as well. Famous for its world-renowned Ice Castle Skating Rink, the village at Blue Jay also offers shops, dining, a cinema complex and numerous hiking trails.

Nearby, Santa's Village in Skyforest is an enchanting park especially popular among the younger set. Open from June through February, attractions include visits with Santa, a petting zoo, puppet shows, rides and reindeer.

Just east of Santa's Village is the Arboretum Trail, an informative self-guided mile-long tour through the forest among the deciduous, conifer and redwood trees.

At Running Springs one approaches Southern California's premier ski country. Snow Valley with a top elevation of 7,841 feet and a vertical rise of 1,141 feet, all accessible by 12 chairlifts, affords challenging terrain for the advanced skier as well as "bunny slopes" for beginners.

South of Snow Valley (formerly Fish Camp) Ski area and east of Running Springs is the National Childrens' Forest. Created in the wake of a devasting fire, which destroyed 53,000 acres of brush and timber, today a self-guided nature trail explores the successful reforestation of this once ravaged mountainscape.

Fire Lookout Towers are open at Strawberry Peak near Rim Forest and Keller Peak near Running Springs. Each afford spectacular views during daylight hours in the summer months.

Just beyond the village of Arrowbear, Green Valley Lake offers sport fishing in the summer and downhill and cross-country skiing during the winter months.

Lake Silverwood (1,000 acres) northwest of Arrowhead, just below the beautiful Valley of Enchantment and Cedar Pines Park, permits public boat launching. Damming the headwaters of the Mojave River, this vast water playground thus created is a popular vacation destination among boating enthusiasts.

Elsewhere, Lake Gregory, referred to by locals as "little

THE NATIONAL CHILDREN'S FOREST LOCATED WITHIN THE SAN BERNARDINO NATIONAL FOREST WAS DESIGNED AND DEVELOPED FOR VERY SPECIAL GUESTS, AND TO TELL A SPECIAL STORY. CHILDREN, INCLUDING THOSE VISUALLY HANDICAPPED OR CONFINED TO A WHEEL CHAIR, WILL BE ABLE TO ENJOY SOME OF THE WONDERS OF NATURE IN THIS 20 ACRE AREA. THE STORY IS OF LIFE, HOPE, AND THE FUTURE.

THIS TINY FOREST IS NOT LOCATED IN THE MOST SCENIC PART OF THIS LARGE NATIONAL FOREST, BUT IN AN AREA THAT BEARS THE UGLY SCARS OF A TRAGIC FOREST FIRE. CREATING A CHILDREN'S FOREST IN SUCH A PLACE WAS INTENTIONAL AND FORMS THE BASIS FOR OUR STORY.

EARLY ON THE MORNING OF NOVEMBER 13, 1970, VIOLENT WINDS BLEW EMBERS FROM A CAMPFIRE INTO A PATCH OF DRY BRUSH. THIS UNLEASHED THE MOST DEVASTATING FIRE IN THE HISTORY OF THIS NATIONAL FOREST. THE WIND-WHIPPED FLAMES SPREAD THROUGH THE FOREST AT AN AMAZING SPEED, AND AT TIMES THEY DEVOURED AN ACRE EACH SECOND. OVER 3,000 MEN FOUGHT FOR SIX DAYS TO BRING THIS MONSTER UNDER CONTROL. FINALLY, A BLANKET OF SNOW HELPED END THE DAMAGE SUFFERED BY THE FOREST. WHEN IT WAS ALL OVER, 53,000 ACRES OF LAND LAY IN CHARRED RUINS.

MOUNTAIN LIVING
BIG BEAR LAKE

QUAKING ASPEN

ONE OF THE MOST COLORFUL OF HIGH-MOUNTAIN TREES. A SLENDER, IRREGULARLY BRANCHED DENDROID, AND ONE USUALLY FOUND IN CLOSE STANDS ON SLOPES AND MOUNTAIN FLATS. THE ASPEN'S GREEN-WHITE TRUNKS WITH DULL-GREEN SUMMER LEAVES THAN TURN YELLOW IN THE AUTUMN CREATE A SPECTACULAR VISTA. ITS FLATTENED LEAF STALKS CAUSE THE LEAVES TO FLUTTER IN THE BREEZE, A READILY RECOGNIZABLE CHARACTERISTIC OF THE "QUAKING" ASPEN.

Switzerland," is frequented by sunbathers, sport fishermen and those preferring a more languid lake experience.

Fishermen will find Arrowhead, Silverwood, and Gregory all stocked with trout, catfish, crappie, blue gill, bass, and an occasional salmon.

Big Bear's beautiful blue lake set amidst pine forests, ringed by privately owned cabins and (because of underwater springs) rarely frozen serves as the focal point for recreational pursuits in the San Bernardino high country. Three communities line its 22-mile shoreline, each catering to the sports enthusiast, and there are indeed opportunities for nearly all outdoor pursuits. Waterskiing in the summer, snowskiing in the winter, backpacking in the extensive San Gorgonio Wilderness, hunting, and fishing; the list seems endless.

In the city of Big Bear Lake, scenic boat tours leave historic Pine Knot Landing for 80-minute excursions throughout spring, summer, and early fall. Narrated commentary provides background on Big Bear Dam, Treasure Island, the Solar Observatory and other historical points of interest. (Operated by the California Institute of Technology in Pasadena, Big Bear Solar Observatory is open to the public on Saturdays.) Seasonal boating on Big Bear Lake is one of the most popular activities at the resort. Powerboats, rowboats, sailboats, canoes, and kayaks traverse the lake along with sail boarders and jet skiers. There are nine launching and rental sites around the lake including Big Bear Marina and Boulder Bay Marina. Recently the city of Big Bear Lake opened a swimming beach.

Trailheads around the lake lead eager naturalists into the beauty of the Alpen wilderness. Castle Rock and Cougar Crest Trails are among the more popular. A World Champion Lodgepole Pine standing 110-feet high is located south of Big Bear Lake where it dominates the landscape. Largest known lodgepole pine in the world, it contains enough lumber to build three average-size houses. Other extraordinary sights are to be enjoyed at Big Falls where water plummets 500 feet down San Gorgonio Moun-

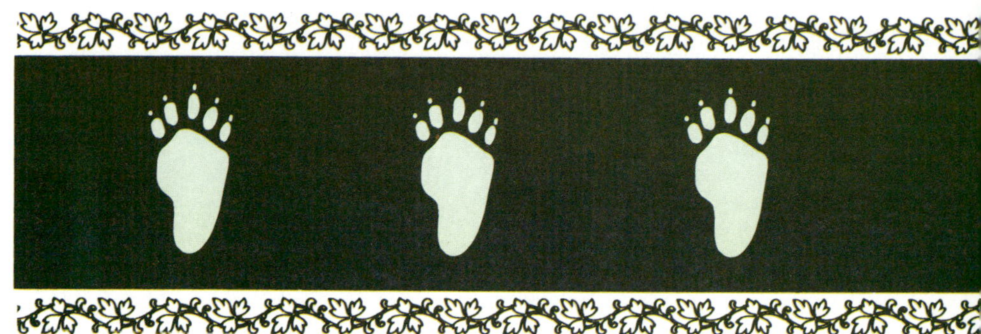

tain in beautiful cascades. Check with the Big Bear Ranger Station for directions and back-country wilderness permits.

For younger visitors, the Magic Mountain Alpine Slide consists of controlled sled rides down a mountainside. A scenic chairlift takes riders to the top of the slide. Big Bear Lake also has its own zoo—Moonridge Animal Park. The zoo contains animals representative of the area: Black Bear, golden eagles, mountain lions, and deer.

A year-round resort, Big Bear offers downhill or *alpine* snow skiers three excellent choices—Bear Mountain (elevation 8,600 feet), Snow Forest, and the ever-popular Snow Summit (with an elevation of 8,200 feet). Extensive use of snow-making equipment and illuminated slopes have made day and night skiing in the San Bernardino Mountains tremendously popular for Southern Californians. Increasingly, cross-country or *Nordic* skiing gains in popularity.

Overnight camping is available at such places as Big Pine Flat, Holcomb Valley, Grout Bay, and Pineknot. Picnicking is popular at Aspen Glen, Big Bear City Park, and Meadows Edge. Hiking, golfing, horseback riding, hunting, and fishing are all available within the Big Bear Lake area.

Annual events on the area's calendar include Old Miners' Days in late July with barbecues, burro races, street dances, and a Miss Clementine Contest; Big Bear's Spring Fling with fishing derbies and boat regattas; and the Oktoberfest with its polka dances and German foods

Shopping throughout the Big Bear Lake vicinity will uncover a wide range of goods and services from the ordinary to the exotic. The area's restaurants and lodges, hotels and condominiums uphold a tradition of hospitality that dates back more than a century.

Near Big Bear is Holcomb Valley, scene of the 1860's gold strike. Two bustling boom towns once occupied these parts. Today whispering pines and memories are about all that remain. The Holcomb Valley Gold Fever Trail is a 2- to 3-hour self-guided auto tour through Holcomb Valley. Several historic sites are marked. Of particular interest is Two Gun Bill's Saloon, Hangman's Tree, and Wilbur's Grave. Guidebooks are available at local bookshops as well as at the Big Bear Ranger Station.

The Ponderosa and Whispering Pines Nature Trails in nearby Barton Flats are self-guided walking tours and cover easily managed terrain. Numerous descriptions of shrubs, trees, and landforms align the trail. Guideropes and descriptions in Braille help accommodate blind visitors. Not far away, Jenks Lake is one of the area's more popular "fishing holes."

"HIGH ON THE MOUNTAINS ABOVE THE MOJAVE LIVE BOBCATS, DEER, AND NORTH AMERICA'S RAREST BIGGAME ANIMAL, THE DESERT BIGHORN. ONE DAY, WHILE OUT HIKING, I HAD THE LUCK TO SEE BIGHORN. A RAM WITH ELEGANT CURLED HORNS PERCHED ON A ROCK CLIFF, ALONGSIDE A EWE AND YEARLING. CURIOUS AND CAUTIOUS, THEY WATCHED ME AS CLOSELY AS I WATCHED THEM. THE RAM BOLDLY VENTURED TO THE CREEK FOR WATER. THEN ALL THREE BOUNDED UP THE CLIFFS AND DISAPPEARED."

—SUZANNE VENINO
NATIONAL GEOGRAPHIC

HOLCOMB VALLEY

BIG BEAR stands considerably higher than the surrounding mountain valleys. Consequently it garners more of the "white stuff." Here winter sports are paramount where an abundance of snow annually transforms this high country destination into a true winter wonderland.

TONY KERST

MARK E. GIBSON

MARK E. GIBSON

DON JONES

OLD LOGGING ROADS penetrate much of these mountains, making their alpine beauty accessible to even the most urbanized mountaineer. Towns such as Running Springs (far right) and Idyllwild (right), born in and around the sawmills of the past, today cater to tourism and outdoor sports enthusiasts.

ADAM COLLINGS

ROY MURPHY

MARK E GIBSON

MARK E. GIBSON

Overhead, 11,502-foot San Gorgonio Mountain rises above the forests and canyons. "Old Greyback" as it is called by locals, forms the centerpiece for the 55,000-acre San Gorgonio Wilderness. On its north face, steep-walled basins and uniform piles of loose rock — cirques and moraines — attest to the prehistoric presence of Ice Age glaciers.

SAN GORGONIO TROUT

o the north, beyond Cajon Pass, the Alps acquire another name, San Gabriel, in honor of the Spanish mission settlement established at the foot of these mountains some 200 years ago. The San Gabriels are the heart of 700,000-acre Angeles National Forest, 36,000 acres of which make up the San Gabriel Wilderness. Angeles Crest Highway (State Highway 2) runs along much of the San Gabriel Range, connecting with Highway 138, desert gateway to Arrowhead Mountain, at Cajon Pass.

Wrightwood, a piney village bridging high desert and high country in the San Gabriels is center for mountain commerce and recreational pursuits. Mountain High, a trendy ski resort popular among Angelenos (residents of Los Angeles) is located here as are charming eateries, galleries and outdoor sports outfiftters. Above towers 10,500-foot Mt. San Antonio (locals call it Old Baldy due to its barren, timberless summit).

At Big Pines, the Angeles National Forest dispenses information and mountain bulletins from its ranger station located here. Wilderness permits can be obtained free of charge for those wishing to camp overnight in the back country. Tiny Jackson Lake is one of several popular camping destinations in the area that do not require permits.

Further along the Angeles Crest Highway spectacular rugged mountainscapes dominate every vista. This is bighorn sheep country. The San Gabriel Wilderness is also home to bear, deer, and mountain lion.

Camp Buckhorn is beautiful and woodsy. Giant Incense cedars tower above its fern-laden canyon, and popular campsites.

At Chilao, an outstanding Visitors Center (finest of any National Forest in the country) houses informative, entertaining exhibits. Guest facilities, campgrounds and miles of nature trails through forests and meadows are available here.

Beyond, Angeles Crest Highway skirts Mount Wilson, with its famed Observatory, to drop dramatically into the sea of cities that is Los Angeles.

Where high desert meets low desert, at San Gorgonio Pass, stately Mt. San Jacinto thrusts skyward. This is a spectacular landscape of granite, pine-clad peaks piercing the heavens. Desert tones are muted, and pastel, set off against a sky of intense blue. Natural palm-lined oasis here have been converted into world famous resorts known collectively as Palm Springs (or simply, The Springs).

To fully capture the majesty of the place one should definitely indulge in a trip on the Palm Springs Aerial Tramway. This world-famous tram whisks guests more than 8,500 feet from desert floor to mountaintop, literally from palms to pines, in a mere 20 minutes. Atop, amid an alpine setting, you can enjoy the Bavarian lodge or strike out on a hiking adventure in the back country of the San Jacinto Wilderness. The Desert View Trail will provide not only excellent views of the Colorado Desert, but also of the high mountain country with granite peaks rising over 10,000 feet. The self-guided Nature Trail leads you along a pleasant stroll through forests and meadows. For the more experienced hikers there are many miles of trails which penetrate the wilderness. Inquire at the Ranger Station located here for maps and information on overnight camping. Free permits, required for all hiking in the San Jacinto Wilderness, can be obtained at the Ranger Station.

From Palm Dėsert take scenic Palms to Pines Highway to picturesque Idllywild and Lake Hemet. A popular base camp for backpackers and rock climbers, Idyllwild, with its rustic mountain homes and ranches and informative visitor center, serves as a gateway to Mt. San Jacinto.

PYGMY NUTHATCH

IDYLLWILD SCHOOL OF MUSIC AND THE ARTS HAS PROVIDED A QUALITY SUMMER PROGRAM IN THEATER, DANCE, MUSIC AND ART FOR 37 YEARS.

IN 1950, MAX AND BEE KRONE OPENED THE SCHOOL WITH THE PURPOSE OF GIVING PEOPLE OF ALL AGES THE OPPORTUNITY TO STUDY THE VISUAL AND PERFORMING ARTS IN IDYLLWILD'S BEAUTIFUL SETTING.

SITUATED ON A 205-ACRE CAMPUS AT THE END OF TOLL GATE ROAD, ISOMATA'S CONCERTS, PERFORMANCES AND ART SHOWS ARE SCHEDULED FROM JUNE THROUGH SEPTEMBER OF EACH YEAR.

GUMPERTZ/BENTLEY/FRIED

Man's presence in these Alps of Southern California has brought about a significant impact upon this fragile alpine environment. Today, while much remains natural and protected from all development, thousands now live and play here in the forest.

BIG BEAR CHAMBER OF COMMERCE

LAKE ARROWHEAD HILTON LODGE

BIG BEAR CHAMBER OF COMMERCE

BIG BEAR INN

ROY MURPHY

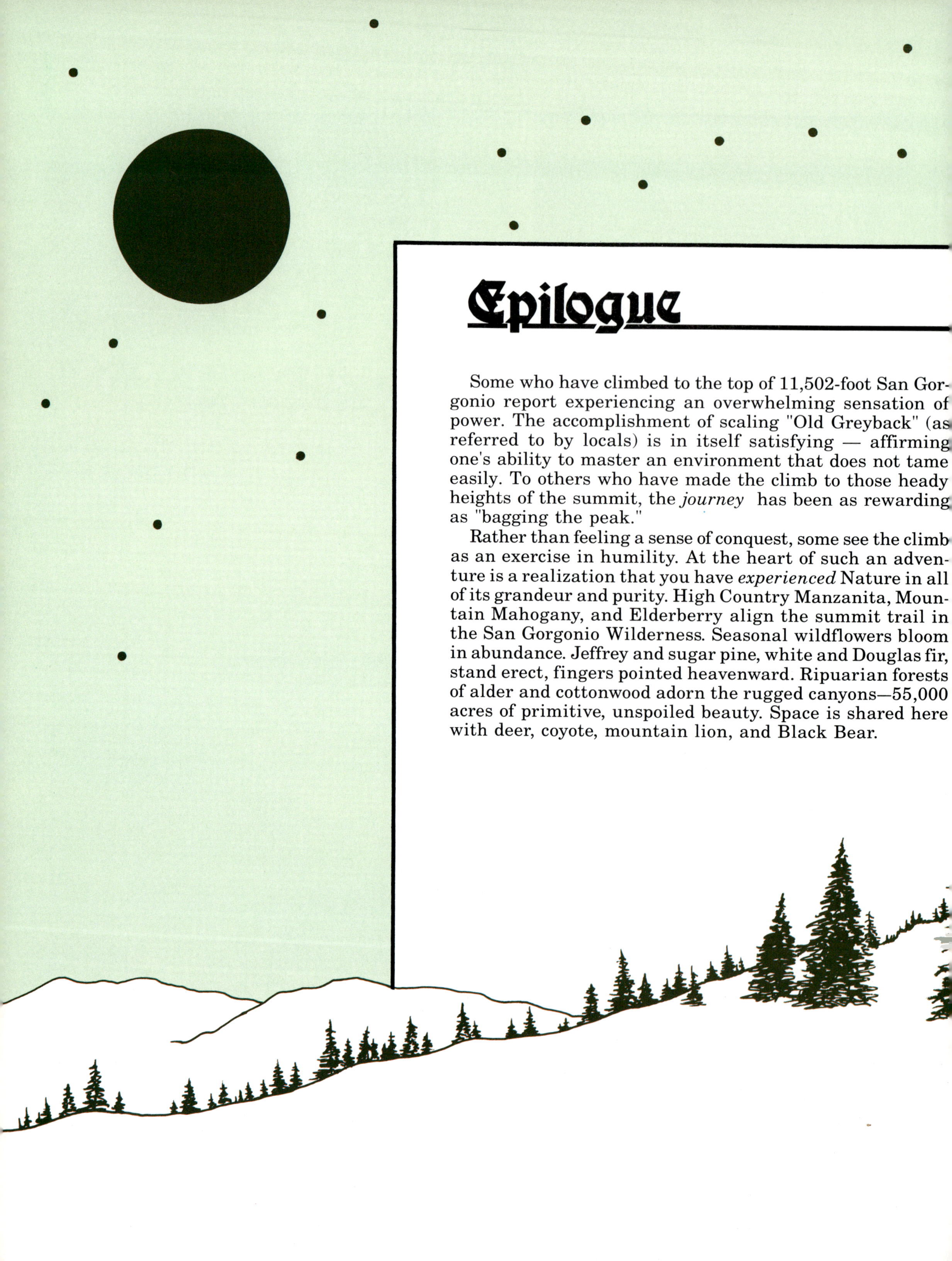

Epilogue

Some who have climbed to the top of 11,502-foot San Gorgonio report experiencing an overwhelming sensation of power. The accomplishment of scaling "Old Greyback" (as referred to by locals) is in itself satisfying — affirming one's ability to master an environment that does not tame easily. To others who have made the climb to those heady heights of the summit, the *journey* has been as rewarding as "bagging the peak."

Rather than feeling a sense of conquest, some see the climb as an exercise in humility. At the heart of such an adventure is a realization that you have *experienced* Nature in all of its grandeur and purity. High Country Manzanita, Mountain Mahogany, and Elderberry align the summit trail in the San Gorgonio Wilderness. Seasonal wildflowers bloom in abundance. Jeffrey and sugar pine, white and Douglas fir, stand erect, fingers pointed heavenward. Ripuarian forests of alder and cottonwood adorn the rugged canyons—55,000 acres of primitive, unspoiled beauty. Space is shared here with deer, coyote, mountain lion, and Black Bear.

It is fitting that at such a place, deep in the heart of the wilderness, one's thoughts turn to the personal attachment that each of us as living beings have to Mother Earth.

The first race of man here, the Native American Indians, lived simple lives. They hunted, fished, organized their communities, and lived out their lives while enjoying a oneness with the land that has never before or since been equalled.

Today few corners of these mountains have escaped exploitation. The Southwest's largest population of bighorn sheep still roam its backcountry and some groves of virgin fir and pine stand untouched, never before logged, in remote canyons and corners of the woods. Yet, unquestionably much has been lost. Lost, but not irretrievable so.

The great, granite mountains themselves stand unaffected. From the Shoshone to the urbanite they remain as ever, timeless and silent. It is the delicate world of the forest, meadow, lake, and open woodland that today stands jeopardized.

Elements of life here in the mountains of Southern California are centered around cherished memories of an existence long since past. Smog frequently shrouds Little Bear Valley, pulled upward as if though the flue of a chimney, into the heights where it stunts the growth of the ponderosa pine. Elk no longer roam the foothills, and sighting a deer in and around mountain communities has become a rare event. Yet those who live here care, as do many of those who look longingly towards these mountains from the metropolis below. As a result of this heartfelt concern, born of love for a place, change is in the offing.

With millions of dollars and hours of exhaustive study expended, air quality has and continues to improve in the Los Angeles Basin, thus alleviating the once frequent stress it placed on the island forests above that basin.

Strict hunting and land use regulations await the common consensus to protect native wildlife populations while efforts to reintroduce species since eradicated from these alps have begun.

The planting of new forests to heal scars left by fires and clear-cut logging has been long in coming here, where a fragile ecosystem cannot restore itself without man's assistance. Finally that aid has begun.

John Muir lobbied long and hard on behalf of efforts to protect the unspoiled grandeur of Nature's wild places. Today a new type of concerned American devotes energies and imagination to restoration; bringing back former grandeur to regions that have since been exhausted, having given all, while suffering greatly, that man might enjoy an affluent, comfortable existence.

The mountains of Southern California with their deep, forested valleys, jeweled lakes, and remote high country are among the most widely visited in the United States. The mile-high lake resorts and year-round recreational areas of Arrowhead and Big Bear are leading the entire region into the twenty-first century. To the people who make these communities their home, and to those who visit these special places, the challenges of the future are many. Some challenges seem on the surface to contradict one another — the urbanization *and* conservation of forest lands; resort development *and* the preservation of wilderness. Such conflicts afford extraordinary opportunities to further enhance a geographical area, unlike any in this country, in such a way that generations who follow will know how deeply we cared.

INDEX

**Type in boldface indicates photograph or illustration.*

ACKNOWLEDGEMENTS

No project as involved as the production and publication of a new book is ever completed without the contributions of time, talent and financial resources from many dedicated individuals. ARROWHEAD-BIG BEAR/the alps of southern California is the result of such an effort. Special thanks goes to our Art Director, Mr. David Brzowski.

We wish to also express our appreciation to Mr. Richard Farrell of Lake Arrowhead, Mr. Tim Wood of Big Bear, Dr. Paul Rizzo and Dr. Sheila Moore of Big Bear and to the Big Bear Chamber of Commerce — to photographers and illustrators (herein credited) who have remained supportive throughout the duration of this project — to production and backup staff — and to Divine Providence always.

ADAM RANDOLPH COLLINGS
incorporated

B-24
Pine Clad Shores of Big Bear Lake
"Rim o' the World Drive," San Bernardino Mountains, Calif.